SECONDARY SCHOOL ADMISSIONS PREP: THE ESSENTIALS

Version 2020-2021

TABLE OF CONTENTS

OVERVIEW

SSAP Timelines

These are suggestions for a timeline for this process. This process is different for everyone, so this is not a one-size-fits-all timeline. The diagnostic score will be a clear indicator of how much time is needed for preparation.

<u>For students who are home for the summer</u>:

May - June
- Student takes a diagnostic
- Have a post-diagnostic meeting or call. Build a plan for the student.
- If the child needs accommodations, the proper paperwork is gathered for the test they will take.
  - Students will need a current neuropsychological evaluation for the specific test from within the last three years. Their school will also need to submit supporting documentation in order for the accommodations to be processed. Students can register only after accommodations have been approved.

June - August
- Use the summer to begin prep work.
  - Focus on fundamental Math content.
  - Focus on developing a consistent Vocabulary practice.
- The tutor and student will focus on putting the fundamentals in place. The student will learn how to breaking down the standardized test questions.

*July 31st - ISEE Registration Opens
- Register for two tests; we recommend November (fall test season) and December (winter test season)

August - September
- Begin the practice test process:
  - The student should come in to take the first practice test since the diagnostic. Taking it earlier is fine, too.
  - The student should take a practice test approximately once a month.
    - This suggestion is student-dependent. Tutors and Directors should communicate about a plan that caters to the specific needs and timeline of each student.
- The tutor and student will focus on approaching the test as a whole:
  - They will learn how to pace their work and optimize their strengths in the midst of taking a test.
  - Full test sections will be assigned as homework for the student to practice taking full sections on their own under timed conditions.
  - The tutor and student will continue to address content gaps as they that arise.
  - Use the score report from each practice test to adjust the frequency and focus of lessons as needed.

- Performance Prep tools will help to reduce anxiety and will cultivate a strong test-taking mindset.

October
- The practice test process and work between the tutor and student continues.
- SSAT: Have the student take an October test, with the understanding that this is the first of two tests. This is part of the "practice round."

November
- The practice test process and work between the tutor and student continues.
- ISEE: Have the student take the November test:
  - Use the score report from each practice test to adjust the frequency and focus of lessons as needed.
- SSAT: Have the student take the November test:
  - Allow the score report from each practice test to adjust the frequency and focus of lessons as needed.
- Stay up to date with families regarding the results of each test:
  - Adjust the frequency and focus of lessons as needed.
- Students should share their official score reports with their tutor.

December - January
- ISEE: Have the student take the December test.
  - Stay up to date with families regarding the results of each test.

For students who are away for the summer

March - April
- The student takes a diagnostic.
- Have a meeting or call to review the diagnostic. Build a plan for the student.
  - SSAT: If a student comes in below a 65th percentile and the intent is to aim for the 85th percentile, **it is important to begin preparation before the summer break.**
  - ISEE: If a student comes in below a 5 stanine and the intent is to aim for a 7 stanine, **it is important to begin preparation before the summer break .**
- If the child needs accommodations, proper paperwork must be gathered for the test they will take
  - They will need a current neuropsychological evaluation for the specific test from within the last three years. Their school will also need to submit supporting documentation in order for the accommodations to be processed.
  - **Students cannot register for the test until the accommodations are approved.**

May - June
- Use the spring to begin prep work.
  - Focus on Fundamental Math Content.
  - Focus on developing a consistent Vocabulary Practice.
- The tutor and student will put the fundamental Math content and vocabulary practice in place and work on navigating and breaking down the standardized test questions.

July - Early August
- This is often a holiday.
  - It is very normal to take the month off and resume work in August.
- Continuing light practice can help to achieve and maintain consistency during the holiday.
- Remote tutoring is an option.
- We are also happy to provide clear suggestions for summer practice focused on fundamental concepts.
- *July 31st - ISEE registration opens.
  - Registration fills up fast. Don't wait. We highly recommend registering on the first day.
  - Register for two tests. We recommend November (fall test season) and December (winter test season)

August - September
- Begin the practice test process.
  - Make sure the student takes the first practice test since the diagnostic.

- It's completely okay if a student wants to take the first test earlier.
  - Have the student take a practice test approximately once a month.
    - For the ISEE there are only two shots, and sometimes only one. We want to address all test-taking issues before the real exam.
    - This suggestion is student-dependent. Each student has specific needs. Building a plan that is specific to the student's needs is a significant part of our approach.
- The tutor and student will work on approaching the test as a whole. They will
  - work on pacing the student's work and optimizing test-taking strengths.
  - build from drills to full test sections practice for homework as a way of learning the skills required for test-taking.
  - continue to address content gaps as they arise.
  - use the score report from each practice test to adjust the frequency and focus of lessons, as needed.
  - rely on Performance Prep tools in sessions to cultivate a strong test-taking mindset and reduce anxiety.

October
- The practice test process and work between the tutor and student continue.
- Possible action:
  - SSAT: If a student is on track with preparation, take the October test as the first of two practice tests. This is part of the "practice round."

November
- The practice test process and work between the tutor and student continue.
  - Allow the score report from each practice test to adjust the frequency and focus of lessons, as needed.
- ISEE: Have the student take the November test.
- SSAT: Have the student take the November test.

December - January
- ISEE: Have the student take the December test.

ISEE

Description/Demographic
- An exam offered by the ERB for acceptance into private primary and secondary schools.
- Lower Level: applying to 5th and 6th grades
- Middle Level: applying to 7th and 8th grades
- Upper Level: applying to 9th through 12th grades

Length
- Lower Level: about 2½ hours
- Upper and Middle Levels: about 3 hours
- Can be taken once per testing season: Fall (August-November), winter (December-March), and spring/summer (April-July).

Scoring
- Four options for every answer; no guessing penalty
- Scoring: scaled score →percentile→stanine
  Stanines are determined based on the following percentiles:

1—1%-3%	6—60%-76%
2—4%-10%	7—77%-88%
3—11%-22%	8—89%-95%
4—23%-39%	9—96%-99%
5—40%-59%	

- A 5th stanine is designed to be average. Scores above this level may help a student gain admission to a given school, and scores below may hinder that student.

Content
Upper/Middle

Section	Time Allowed	Number of Questions
Verbal Reasoning	20 minutes	20 synonym questions, 20 sentence-completion questions
Quantitative Reasoning	35 minutes	37 questions
Reading Comprehension	35 minutes	36 questions (6 passages)
Mathematics Achievement	40 minutes	47 questions
Essay	30 minutes	1 prompt

Lower

Section	Time Allowed	Number of Questions
Verbal Reasoning	20 minutes	17 synonym questions, 17 sentence-completion questions
Quantitative Reasoning	35 minutes	38 questions
Reading Comprehension	25 minutes	25 questions (5 passages)

Mathematics Achievement	30 minutes	30 questions
Essay	30 minutes	1 prompt

SSAT

Description/Demographic

- Used for acceptance into private secondary schools. The SSAT tends to be a more popular option for students applying to boarding schools.
- Can be taken as many times as it is offered.
- Schools will see if a student has taken the test more than once but will only receive the full score report that the student chooses to send.
- Elementary: applying to 4th and 5th grades
- Middle Level: applying 6th, 7th, or 8th grade
- Upper Level: applying to 9th through 12th grades

Length

This test runs about 3 hours.

Scoring

- There are five options for every answer, and a guessing penalty of a quarter of a point for each incorrect answer.
- Raw score → scaled score (based on a curve using the last few years of a student's performance) → percentile
- A highly competitive score for an 8th grader is at or above the 85th percentile.

Content

Section	Time Allowed	Number of Questions
Writing Sample	25 minutes	Upper: students choose from 1 creative prompt and 1 essay prompt; Middle: students choose from 2 creative prompts.
Quantitative	30 minutes	25 questions
Reading	40 minutes	40 questions (approximately 7 passages)
Verbal	30 minutes	30 synonym questions, 30 analogy questions
Quantitative	30 minutes	25 questions
Experimental Section*	15 minutes	16 questions

While the content of the questions themselves varies between the Upper and Middle levels, the breakdown, timing, and number of questions in each section do not.

*Note also that some administrations (but not all) of the SSAT include a 16-question experimental section, which is not scored.

Catholic High School Entrance Exams

Description/Demographic

- The TACHS, HSPT, and COOP are three tests given for entrance into parochial secondary schools.
- These tests are usually administered on one or two specific days at various parochial schools.
- The TACHS is developed by The Riverside Publishing Company. The HSPT is developed by STS. The COOP serves students applying to parochial schools in Long Island and northern New Jersey.

Length

The tests run approximately 2½ to 3 hours. There is typically one test date offered that all students must attend.

Scoring

COOP

Raw score → scaled score → local and national percentiles

HSPT

Raw score → scaled score between 200 and 800
A percentile is also reported.

TACHS

Raw score → scaled score → percentile

Content

COOP

Section	Time Allowed	Number of Questions
Sequences	17 minutes	20 questions
Analogies	12 minutes	20 questions
Quantitative Reasoning	40 minutes	20 questions
Verbal Reasoning – Words	23 minutes	20 questions
Verbal Reasoning – Context	22 minutes	20 questions
Reading and Language Arts	62 minutes	41 questions
Mathematics	40 minutes	25 questions

HSPT

Section	Time Allowed	Number of Questions
Verbal	16 minutes	60 questions
Quantitative	30 minutes	52 questions
Reading	25 minutes	62 questions
Mathematics	45 minutes	64 questions
Language	20 minutes	60 questions

TACHS

Section	Time Allowed (*approximate*)	Number of Questions (*approximate*)
Reading: Vocabulary	10 minutes	20 questions
Reading: Comprehension	25 minutes	30 questions
Language: Mechanics	23 minutes	40 questions
Language: Paragraphs	7 minutes	10 questions
Math: Concepts	33 minutes	32 questions
Math: Estimation	7 minutes	18 questions
Ability: Similarities and Changes	25 minutes	40 questions
Ability: Abstract Reasoning	7 minutes	10 questions

Hunter

Description/Demographic

- Very little information is made public about the test itself, although it is the primary criterion for admission to the school.
- This test is offered in early January for the school year beginning the following fall.
- The test is administered to 6th-grade students, as 7th grade is the one-and-only point of entry into Hunter. 6th-grade students are only eligible for the entrance exam if they have achieved a scaled score of 700 or higher on the 5th-grade New York State ELA test, and a score of 714 or higher on the corresponding 5th-grade New York State math test. (If applying out from a private or parochial school, 5th-grade standardized test scores must be in or above the 90th percentile.)

Length

The test runs approximately 3 hours. There is one sole test date each year, and neither make-up dates nor rescheduling are made available, unless in case of inclement weather.

Scoring

- The multiple-choice sections are computer-scored and hand-checked for accuracy. A cut-off score is established, allowing the top 500 scorers to have their essays read by a panel of HCHS English faculty. The 170 students with the best essays are selected for admission to HCHS.
- HCHS also maintains a wait list of 25 to 30 students. If admitted students decline admission or withdraw from HCHS prior to the beginning of 7th grade, students from the wait list are offered admission, at HCHS's discretion.

Content

Section	Time Allowed	Number of Questions
English Language Arts	20 minutes	60 questions
Mathematics	35 minutes	35 questions
Writing Assignment	35 minutes	1 prompt

Students have 3 hours to complete the entire test, without specific time restraints for any section.

SHSAT

Description/Demographic

The SHSAT is administered to 8th- and 9th-graders who are New York City residents seeking placement in one of the public magnet schools in New York, including:

- Bronx High School of Science
- Brooklyn Technical High School
- High School of Mathematics, Science and Engineering at City College
- High School of American Studies at Lehman College
- Queens High School for the Sciences at York College
- Stuyvesant High School
- Brooklyn Latin*
- Staten Island Technical High School (newly designated)*

The SHSAT is the only factor of admission into these high schools, and the acceptance rate hovers around 15%. (Note: for those schools marked with an asterisk, the SHSAT is not required, and other criteria are considered.)

SHSAT testing is open to public district and charter school students, private and parochial school students, students with disabilities, students with limited mobility, and English Language Learners (ELLs). Students are issued a Test Ticket, which will indicate the date, time and location of the test, as well any applicable testing accommodations. Students must test on the specified date and at the assigned location. This will be the only chance to take the exam.

Length

The test must be completed within 3 hours.
The test is self-paced; the proctor will not prompt the student to move to the next section.

The SHSAT has two sections: English Language Arts (ELA) and Math. Each section consists of 57 questions: 47 scored questions and 10 embedded field test questions.

The student will NOT know which questions are scored and which are field test questions. It is to the student's advantage to answer all questions in each section.

Scoring

- Raw scores → scaled scores a maximum possible score of 800.
- No guessing penalty.
- Scaled scores are based on the number of questions that the student answered correctly, combined with the difficulty level of the questions. Students receive scaled scores for the verbal and mathematics sections of the test, which are added together to make their composite score.
- After scores are released to the schools in March, students and their parents may review the results of their examination by requesting an appointment with a Department of Education assessment specialist.

Content

Section	Number of Questions
Verbal: Revising/Editing	9–11 questions
Verbal: Reading Comprehension	46–48 questions
Mathematics	57 questions

It is important to note that unlike most other standardized tests, the SHSAT allows students to budget their own time.

Revising/Editing Section

The Revising/Editing section assesses a student's ability to recognize and correct language errors and improve the overall quality of the writing.
- In Part A, each question is based on its own sentence/paragraph.
- In Part B, all questions are based on a single, multi-paragraph text.

Reading Comprehension

The Reading Comprehension section assesses a student's ability to understand, analyze, and interpret texts from a variety of genres. The format includes 6 texts, including informational and literary, followed by 6–10 questions.

- Informational texts:
  - May include exposition, argument, and functional text in the form of personal essays, speeches, opinion pieces, essays about art or literature, biographies, memoirs, journalism, and historical, scientific, technical, or economic accounts written for a broad audience.

- Literary texts:
  - May include poetry, adventure stories, historical fiction, mysteries, myths, science fiction, realistic fiction, allegories, parodies, or satire.

Math Section

The Math section consists of word and computational questions in either a multiple-choice or grid-in format. There are five grid-in Math questions and 52 multiple-choice questions.

- Math questions on the Grade 8 test forms are based on material included in the New York City curriculum through Grade 7.

- Math questions on the Grade 9 test forms are based on material through Grade 8.

VOCABULARY

Vocabulary List

Lower Level: Key Words to Know

Abundant	Harmony
Accomplish	Hesitation
Admire	Hustle
Advise	Lair
Anxious	Lavish
Appealing	Linger
Appreciate	Lofty
Aroma	Luxury
Careless	Mock
Commendable	Moist
Construct	Mold
Cynical	Obscure
Deficient	Peddler
Detract	Quiver
Divulge	Reputation
Eligible	Savor
Emancipate	Somber
Envious	Tragedy
Fashion	Unique
Frigid	Worthy
Gnaw	

Middle Level: Key Words to Know

Abrupt	Grave
Absurdity	Hysteria
Admonish	Idyllic
Alarming	Immortal
Aloof	Incomprehensible
Approximate	Inflate
Aquatic	Insanity
Arid	Lush
Awry	Meander
Castigate	Monarch
Celsius	Oriented
Circumference	Pivotal
Clout	Plummet
Commemorate	Recuperate
Concoct	Reed
Confer	Rigid
Configuration	Rind
Confounded	Sentiment
Conspicuous	Serenity
Convene	Sublime
Corrupt	Surveillance
Deflect	Tarnish
Discern	Tendency
Discombobulated	Terrestrial
Eccentric	Tinged
Elaboration	Uncanny
Executive	Veil
Exploit	Venerate
Fathom	Virtuous
Flourish	

All Levels: Key Words to Know

This list is designed to kick-start verbal prep. It contains words appropriate for students from 4th or 5th grade to high school. Even more important, however, is for students to add to their vocabulary lists based on their reading, both in lessons and outside.

A
Abdicate
Abhor
Abridge
Acclaim
Acrid
Adept
Admonish
Adversary
Aggregate
Agile
Allay
Aloof
Amass
Ambiguous
Ambivalence
Ameliorate
Amenable
Amorphous
Annex
Antagonistic
Antidote
Antipathy
Ascertain
Assail
Astute
Audible
Augment
Auspicious
Austere
Authentic
Avarice

B
Banal
Barrage
Barren
Bellicose
Belligerent
Benevolent
Benign
Bequest

Bizarre
Blatant
Blunder
Bolster
Bourgeois
Brandish
Brazen
Brevity
Brittle
Burgeon
Buttress

C
Cajole
Callous
Candid
Capricious
Cater
Cauterize
Censure
Chagrin
Chasm
Churlish
Coerce
Cohere
Compel
Competent
Complacent
Concise
Concur
Condone
Confer
Confound
Congeal
Congenial
Connoisseur
Contaminate
Contort
Converge
Convict
Copious
Corroborate

Cower
Credible
Crumble
Cunning

D
Daunt
Debilitate
Deft
Deject
Delusion
Deplete
Derelict
Desperate
Deter
Detrimental
Deviate
Dexterity
Didactic
Dignity
Dilute
Disavow
Discrepancy
Disdain
Disguise
Disingenuous
Disparage
Dispel
Dissipate
Distend
Distort
Docile
Domestic
Dormant
Drench
Dubious

E
Edict
Effervescent
Egotist
Elegy

Biased Bilingual	Corroboration Counterfeit	Eloquent Embryonic

Empathy	Fulcrum	Imbue
Emulate	Fundamental	Immaculate
Engage	Furtive	Impasse
Enigma		Imperial
Enigmatic	**G**	Imply
Entrust	Galley	Impudent
Envy	Garner	Inane
Ephemeral	Gaudy	Incisive
Epitome	Gaunt	Incite
Equity	Generic	Incognito
Equivocate	Generous	Inconspicuous
Erratic	Genesis	Incorrigible
Esoteric	Genial	Indifferent
Euphemism	Genre	Indignant
Evade	Genuine	Ineffable
Evict	Germane	Ingenuity
Exasperate	Glean	Ingratiate
Exile	Glib	Ingress
Exploit	Glint	Initiate
Extent	Glutton	Innocuous
Extol	Grandiose	Insinuate
	Gratified	Insipid
F	Gratuitous	Insolent
Facet	Gregarious	Insure
Facile	Grim	Integrity
Fallacy	Grotesque	Intricate
Fallow	Guile	Intuition
Famine	Gullible	Inundated
Fatigue	Gully	Invocation
Feasible	Gusto	Ironic
Feeble		Irrefutable
Feign	**H**	
Feisty	Hackneyed	**J**
Felicity	Hamper	Jaded
Finagle	Haphazard	Jargon
Flaccid	Hasten	Jeer
Flamboyant	Haughty	Jeopardize
Flatter	Hefty	Jest
Fleeting	Hiatus	Jocular
Flotsam	Hideous	Judicious
Flourish	Hilarity	Justify
Fluctuate	Hinder	Juxtapose
Foist	Hoard	
Foolhardy	Homely	**K**
Forge	Hone	Keen

Fortunate	Humane	Kindle
Foster	Hybrid	Kinetic
Fragile	Hyperbole	Knoll
Frank	Hypocrite	Kudos
Frantic		
Fret	**I**	**L**
Frugal	Idiosyncratic	Laconic
Lament	Nonchalant	**Q**
Languid	Noncommittal	Queasy
Laud	Nostalgia	Quip
Lavish	Notorious	Quirk
Leniency	Novel	
Levity	Novice	**R**
Limber	Noxious	Rant
Linger	Nullify	Realm
Listless		Recant
Lofty	**O**	Reciprocal
Loquacious	Obdurate	Redolent
Lucid	Oblivion	Remedy
Lucrative	Obscure	Replete
Lugubrious	Obsequious	Repose
Luminous	Obtuse	Repugnant
Lure	Onerous	Rescind
Lustrous	Onus	Reserve
	Opaque	Resolute
M	Opulent	Rhetoric
Malicious	Oscillate	Ruffle
Malleable	Ostentatious	Rupture
Maxim	Overt	
Meager		**S**
Meander	**P**	Scrutinize
Meddle	Pacify	Sedate
Meek	Palpable	Seditious
Menace	Panacea	Skeptical
Meticulous	Pander	Somber
Mettle	Parity	Sovereign
Mimic	Parsimonious	Sparse
Mirage	Patent	Specify
Miser	Pedantic	Speck
Mitigate	Penchant	Spendthrift
Model	Penitent	Spontaneous
Mollify	Penurious	Sporadic
Moral	Perfunctory	Spurn
Morbid	Peripheral	Squander
Morose	Petulant	Static
Motley	Pilfer	Stature
Muddled	Placate	Steadfast
Muffle	Placid	Stimulus

Mundane	Precise	Stingy
Myriad	Probity	Stoic
	Proclivity	Stringent
N	Prodigal	Subside
Nag	Prodigious	Subtle
Narcissism	Profuse	Succinct
Navigate	Provoke	Sullied
Nebulous	Proximity	Summary
Negate	Prudent	Superfluous
Nepotism	Pugnacious	Surrogate
Nomad	Pulverize	Sycophant
Symbiotic	Vital	
T	Vivacious	
Taciturn	Vivid	
Tact	Voracious	
Tangent	Vow	
Tangible	Vulnerable	
Taper		
Taunt	**W**	
Tenacious	Wane	
Terse	Wanton	
Threadbare	Wax	
Thrive	Weary	
Thwart	Whet	
Timid	Whittle	
Tinge	Wicked	
Toil	Willful	
Totemic	Wily	
Tragedy	Wince	
Tranquil	Wont	
Transient	Wrath	
Trite	Writhe	
Truncate		
Tumultuous	**X**	
Turbulence		
	Y	
U		
Ubiquitous	**Z**	
Unconventional	Zany	
Uncouth	Zealot	
Undermine	Zealous	
Underscore	Zenith	
Uniform	Zest	
Universal		
Unruly		
Uproot		
Urbane		
Usurp		

Utilitarian		
V Vacillate Vend Vendetta Veneration Vernacular Versatile Vibrant Viewpoint Vigilant Vigorous Vindication		

Math Vocabulary List

Understanding the following vocabulary will help students break down word problems and content on the Math sections.

Number Terms

Integer
An integer is a whole number that can be positive, negative, or zero.

Whole Number
Whole numbers include positive integers, along with 0. It does not contain fractions or decimals.

Positive Number
A number that is bigger than zero.

Negative Number
A number that is less than zero.

Even Number
An integer which is "evenly divisible" by two.

Odd Number
An odd number is an integer which is not a multiple of two; a number that, when divided by two, leaves a remainder.

Prime Number
A prime number is a whole number greater than 1 whose only factors are 1 and itself.

Digit
Any of the numerals from 0 to 9, especially when forming part of a number.

Units Digit
The unit digit is the one found in the ones column.

Consecutive Numbers
Consecutive numbers are a series of numbers that follow each other in order
(1, 2, 3, 4).

Distinct Numbers
A distinct number is a number in a set or problem that is not equal to other numbers; a number that is different from other numbers in the set or problem.

Rational Numbers
A rational number can be written as a fraction.
Rational numbers are all real numbers. They can be positive or negative.

Irrational Number
A real number that cannot be written as a simple fraction.

Multiple
A multiple is the result of the multiplication of one number by another number. Multiples of numbers are introduced in the multiplication tables.

Factor
Numbers can be multiplied together to make another number. The numbers that we multiply are the factors of the product.

Terms Used to Make Equations:

Divisible By
A number that can be divided by another number.

Sum
The result of an addition

Difference
The result of a subtraction

Product
The result of a multiplication

Quotient
The result of a division

Remainder
The amount left over when dividing

Rules of Zero

- Zero is neither positive nor negative.
- Zero is even.
- Zero is an integer.
- Zero multiplied by any number is zero.
- Zero divided by any number is zero.
- You cannot divide a number by zero (5/0 = undefined).

Positive and Negative Integers

Adding Integers
- If the signs are the same, add and keep the same sign:
  - (+) + (+) = add the numbers and the answer is positive.
- (-) + (-) = add the numbers and the answer is negative. If the signs are different, subtract the numbers and use the sign of the larger number.
  - (+) + (-) = subtract the numbers and use the sign of the bigger number.
  - (-) + (+) = subtract the numbers and use the sign of the bigger number.

Subtracting Integers
- The sign of the first number stays the same. Change subtraction to addition and change the sign of the second number. Once you have applied this rule, follow the rules for adding integers.
  - (+) – (+) = (+)+(-) then subtract; take the sign of the bigger number.
  - (-) – (-) = (-) + (+) then subtract; take the sign of the bigger number.
  - (+) – (-) = (+) + (+) then add; answer is positive.
  - (-) – (+) = (-) + (-) then add; answer is negative.

Multiplying Integers
- If the signs are the same, multiply or divide and the answer is always positive.
  - (+) multiplied by (+) = (+)
  - (-) multiplied by (-) = (+)
  - (+) divided by (+) = (+)
  - (-) divided by (-) = (+)
- If the signs are different, multiply or divide and the answer is always negative.
  - (+) multiplied by (-) = (-)
  - (-) multiplied by (+) = (-)
  - (+) divided by (-) = (-)
  - (-) divided by (+) = (-)

STUDENT STRATEGIES

Math

Show Your Work

The neater and more organized your work is, the more successful you will be.

Anticipate Answers

Before even reading the answer choices, try answer each question on your own. Then, eliminate answer choices that don't match what you anticipated. The anticipated answer doesn't need to be perfect in order to be useful!

Crossword Method

Try answer the easier questions first and come back to the harder ones later, even if that means skipping a significant number of problems initially.

Remember to Read

Even the math sections of the test involve reading comprehension. The wording of the problems should be studied just as closely as the figures.

Convert the Words

Do your best to turn word problems into mathematical equations or figures. If a question mentions a triangle but does not offer a figure, draw it. If a problem describes an equation in words, write it mathematically.

Think Logic, Not Numbers

Problems frequently require a deeper understanding of the problem itself, not just a solution. Concentrate on more than just the numbers within a problem, and really consider which steps are absolutely necessary in order to solve.

Crossing Out

Physically cross out answer choices on the page for a visual reminder of narrowed down answer choices.

What Do I Know?

When you're stuck, create a written catalog of the information that you *do* know. This is likely to generate some sort of clue to a potential solution.

Plug in Numbers

Particularly in the case of (but not limited to) algebra questions, try to plug in hypothetical numbers and consider the result. This may give you a clue to the next step.

Back solving

If you're at a loss for a plan of attack with a given problem, it can be helpful to consider the answer choices offered and work backward from there.

Do Not Necessarily Solve

Quantitative Comparisons Actually solving for the numbers in each column is frequently unnecessary in order to answer the problem. Before spending valuable time on working out those numbers on paper, make sure that it is absolutely necessary in order to solve the problem.

Beware of Two Variables

Quantitative Comparisons Anything that involves two or more variables should set off a red flag. In many cases, the answer will be that there is not enough information given to determine a relationship between the two columns.
In some cases, however, a problem with two or more variables will offer enough information to determine the values of all the variables involved.

Implementing a System for Math

Some students are much more comforted by structure than others. These students will be much more amenable to the methodology and procedures offered up by the tutor. Students who are more resistant to strategy may have a tougher time with the implementation of a more regimented system and may not be good candidates for this technique.

Step 1: Read the question (and **only** the question).

Step 2: Apply the appropriate strategy (or strategies).

Step 3: Show all your work.
- Write down all calculations and notes necessary to solve the problem in a neat and organized manner.

Step 4: Anticipate an answer.

Step 5: Eliminate unlikely options.
- Using the anticipated answer as a guide, eliminate answer choices that seem to be way off, physically crossing out those choices.

Step 6: Select an answer.

DIVISIBILITY RULES

QUICK REMINDERS:

- All numbers are **divisible by 1**. A number divided by 1 will give the number itself.

- A number is **divisible by 2** if it ends in 0, 2, 4, 6, or 8. These are called *even numbers*.

- A number is **divisible by 5** if it ends in 0 or 5.

- A number is **divisible by 10** if it ends in 0. For example, 56,930 is divisible by 10.

- A number is **divisible by 100** if it ends in "00". For example, 450,000 is divisible by 100.

- A number is **divisible by 1000** if it ends in "000". For example, 450,000 is divisible by 1000.

Let's dig deeper!

Divisibility rules for 3
A number is divisible by 3 if the sum of its digits is divisible by 3 – i.e., if it is a multiple of 3.

Example: Let's look at 308:
- Take the sum of the digits: 3+0+8= 11.
- Check whether the sum is divisible by 3 or not.
- If the sum is a multiple of 3, then the original number is also divisible by 3. Here, since 11 is not divisible by 3, 308 is not divisible by 3, either.

Divisibility by 4
A number is divisible by 4 if the last two digits of a number are divisible by 4 – i.e., if it is a multiple of 4.

Example: Let's look at 2308:
- Add the last two digits 0 and 8.
- 0+8 =8
- 8 is divisible by 4
- This means the original number 2308 is also divisible by 4!

Divisibility by 6

A number is divisible by 6 if the number is also divisible by both 2 and 3. How do we check this? Well, if the last digit of the given number is even AND the sum of its digits is a multiple of 3, then the given number is divisible by 6!

Example: Let's look at 630:
- The number is even, and therefore divisible by 2.
- The sum of its digits is 6+3+0 = 9, which is divisible by 3.
- So, 630 is divisible by 6!

Divisibility rules for 7

Follow the steps below to see if a number is divisible by 7:

- Remove the last digit and multiply it by two.
- Subtract the result of that multiplication from the remaining number.
- Complete the first two steps one more time with the remaining number.
- Is the number 0 or a recognizable 2-digit multiple of 7?
- If yes, the number is divisible by 7.

Example: Let's look at 1073:
- Remove the last digit (3) and double it. This becomes 6.
- Subtract the result (6) from the remaining digits: 107-6 = 101.
- Repeat that process one more time: remove the last digit (1) and double it: 1 x 2 = 2.
- Subtract the result (2) from the remaining digits: 10 – 2 = 8.
- As 8 is not divisible by 7, the number 1073 is not divisible by 7.

Divisibility by 8

If the last three digits of a number are divisible by 8, then the entire number is divisible by 8.

Example: Let's look at 24344:
- Take out the last three digits: 344.
- As 344 is divisible by 8, the original number 24344 is also divisible by 8.

Divisibility by 9

The rule for divisibility by 9 is similar to the rule for by 3. If the sum of the digits is divisible by 9, then the number itself is divisible by 9.

Example: Let's look at 78532
- The sum of its digits (7+8+5+3+2) is 25.
- 25 is not divisible by 9, so 78532 is not divisible by 9.

Divisibility rules for 11

A number is divisible by 11 if the difference of the sum of alternative digits of a number is divisible by 11.

Example: Let's look at 2143:
- Group the alternative digits:
  - Gather the digits which are in odd places together and then gather the digits in even places together. Here 2 & 4 are one group and 1 & 3 are another group.
- Find the sum of each group: 2+4=6 and 1+3= 4
- Find the difference between the two sums: 6-4=2
- If the difference is divisible by 11, then the original number is also divisible by 11. Here, difference is 2, which is not divisible by 11.
- Therefore, 2143 is not divisible by 11.

MATH DRILLS

ADDITION AND SUBTRACTION OF FRACTIONS

In the following 15 problems, add or subtract the fractions as shown. Pay close attention to the signs in each problem. Reduce when necessary. **Show all your work.**

Set A

1) $\frac{1}{2} + \frac{1}{2}$

2) $\frac{1}{3} + \frac{1}{3}$

3) $\frac{1}{4} + \frac{1}{4}$

4) $\frac{2}{3} - \frac{1}{3}$

5) $\frac{3}{4} - \frac{1}{4}$

6) $\frac{5}{6} - \frac{1}{6}$

7) $\frac{1}{2} + \frac{1}{4}$

8) $\frac{1}{3} + \frac{1}{6}$

9) $\frac{1}{2} + \frac{1}{3}$

10) $\frac{3}{4} - \frac{1}{3}$

11) $\frac{2}{3} - \frac{1}{4}$

12) $\frac{1}{8} + \frac{2}{3}$

13) $\frac{5}{8} + \frac{1}{7}$

14) $\frac{7}{9} - \frac{2}{5}$

15) $\frac{5}{6} - \frac{4}{5}$

Set B

1) $\frac{2}{4} + \frac{2}{4}$

2) $\frac{6}{8} - \frac{3}{8}$

3) $\frac{3}{9} + \frac{3}{9}$

4) $\frac{7}{10} - \frac{2}{10}$

5) $\frac{4}{10} + \frac{4}{10}$

6) $\frac{1}{2} + \frac{1}{8}$

7) $\frac{4}{9} - \frac{3}{9}$

8) $\frac{1}{3} + \frac{1}{9}$

9) $\frac{1}{4} + \frac{1}{6}$

10) $\frac{5}{9} + \frac{1}{6}$

11) $\frac{3}{4} - \frac{1}{2}$

12) $\frac{7}{8} - \frac{3}{5}$

13) $\frac{4}{5} - \frac{1}{3}$

14) $\frac{5}{7} - \frac{3}{8}$

15) $\frac{5}{8} + \frac{1}{3}$

MULTIPLICATION AND DIVISION OF FRACTIONS

In the following 15 problems, multiply or divide the fractions as shown. Pay close attention to the signs in each problem. Reduce when necessary. **Show all your work.**

Set A

1) $\frac{1}{2} \times \frac{1}{2}$

2) $\frac{1}{3} \times \frac{1}{3}$

3) $\frac{1}{4} \times \frac{1}{4}$

4) $\frac{2}{3} \div \frac{1}{3}$

5) $\frac{3}{4} \div \frac{1}{4}$

6) $\frac{5}{6} \div \frac{1}{6}$

7) $\frac{1}{2} \times \frac{1}{4}$

8) $\frac{1}{3} \times \frac{1}{6}$

9) $\frac{1}{3} \div \frac{1}{2}$

10) $\frac{1}{2} \div \frac{3}{4}$

11) $\frac{1}{4} \div \frac{2}{3}$

12) $\frac{3}{8} \times \frac{2}{3}$

13) $\frac{4}{5} \div \frac{5}{6}$

14) $\frac{5}{8} \times \frac{1}{7}$

15) $\frac{2}{5} \div \frac{7}{9}$

Set B

1) $\frac{1}{5} \times \frac{1}{5}$

2) $\frac{1}{6} \times \frac{1}{6}$

3) $\frac{2}{3} \times \frac{2}{3}$

4) $\frac{4}{9} \div \frac{2}{9}$

5) $\frac{6}{8} \div \frac{3}{8}$

6) $\frac{7}{10} \div \frac{2}{10}$

7) $\frac{1}{2} \times \frac{1}{8}$

8) $\frac{1}{3} \times \frac{1}{9}$

9) $\frac{1}{4} \times \frac{1}{6}$

10) $\frac{3}{4} \div 1$

11) $\frac{4}{5} \div \frac{1}{3}$

12) $\frac{5}{8} \times \frac{1}{3}$

13) $\frac{5}{9} \div \frac{1}{6}$

14) $\frac{7}{8} \times \frac{3}{5}$

15) $\frac{5}{7} \div \frac{3}{8}$

CONVERTING AN IMPROPER FRACTION TO A MIXED FRACTION

In each of the following 15 problems, convert the improper fraction to a mixed fraction. Reduce the fraction if necessary. **Show all your work.**

Set A

1) $\frac{3}{2}$

2) $\frac{7}{3}$

3) $\frac{12}{5}$

4) $\frac{9}{4}$

5) $\frac{10}{6}$

6) $\frac{4}{1}$

7) $\frac{38}{7}$

8) $\frac{15}{6}$

9) $\frac{45}{10}$

10) $\frac{20}{9}$

11) $\frac{18}{8}$

12) $\frac{11}{3}$

13) $\frac{56}{5}$

14) $\frac{100}{11}$

15) $\frac{502}{50}$

Set B

1) $\frac{5}{4}$

2) $\frac{8}{5}$

3) $\frac{7}{4}$

4) $\frac{3}{1}$

5) $\frac{9}{4}$

6) $\frac{25}{4}$

7) $\frac{10}{3}$

8) $\frac{18}{4}$

9) $\frac{41}{10}$

10) $\frac{49}{6}$

11) $\frac{22}{8}$

12) $\frac{96}{9}$

13) $\frac{23}{11}$

14) $\frac{365}{52}$

15) $\frac{19}{7}$

CONVERTING A MIXED FRACTION TO AN IMPROPER FRACTION

In each of the following 15 problems, convert the mixed fraction to an improper fraction. **Show all your work.**

Set A

1) $1\frac{1}{2}$

2) $3\frac{1}{3}$

3) $4\frac{1}{6}$

4) $1\frac{3}{5}$

5) $2\frac{5}{8}$

6) $3\frac{4}{7}$

7) $8\frac{3}{4}$

8) $10\frac{1}{9}$

9) $2\frac{7}{16}$

10) $4\frac{11}{12}$

11) $6\frac{5}{6}$

12) $12\frac{2}{3}$

13) $15\frac{3}{4}$

14) $9\frac{5}{12}$

15) $17\frac{8}{9}$

Set B

1) 1 ⅓

2) 2 ½

3) 3 ¼

4) 1 ⅝

5) 3 ⅜

6) 4 ⅞

7) 9 ⅔

8) 12 ⅙

9) $2^9/_{12}$

10) $3\ ^{14}/_{15}$

11) 7 ⅞

12) 14 ¾

13) 18 ⅔

14) 4 ¾

15) 112 ⅙

ALGEBRA

In each of the following 15 problems, solve for the unknown. **Show all your work.**

Set A

1) $a + 1 = 3$

2) $z - 1 = 3$

3) $y + 3 = 9$

4) $a - 2 = 5$

5) $5 + b = 17$

6) $5 - c = 3$

7) $2y + 1 = 11$

8) $3z + 6 = 18$

9) $9b - 5 = 22$

10) $8 + 4z = 12$

11) $20 - 5y = 10$

12) $11 + 6w = 29$

13) $44 - 7p = 30$

14) $3 + 10a = 83$

15) $12c - 8 = 100$

Set B

1) $x + 4 = 6$

2) $y - 3 = 7$

3) $z + 3 = 9$

4) $a - 5 = 2$

5) $4 + b = 15$

6) $8 - c = 5$

7) $2x + 3 = 7$

8) $3y + 5 = 20$

9) $8b - 6 = 26$

10) $7 + 3z = 16$

11) $22 - 3x = 7$

12) $13 + 7p = 55$

13) $47 - 6z = 35$

14) $4 + 9b = 76$

15) $14c - 12 = 128$

CROSS MULTIPLICATION

In the following 15 problems, solve for *x*. All answers should be rounded to the nearest hundredth (.01). **Show all work in a neat and organized manner. Use extra paper if necessary.**

Set A

1) $\dfrac{4}{2} = \dfrac{6}{x}$

2) $\dfrac{8}{x} = \dfrac{2}{7}$

3) $\dfrac{x}{2} = \dfrac{20}{4}$

4) $\dfrac{30}{3} = \dfrac{x}{4}$

5) $\dfrac{x}{3} = \dfrac{4}{12}$

6) $\dfrac{15}{5} = \dfrac{x}{3}$

7) $\dfrac{2}{8} = \dfrac{8}{x}$

8) $\dfrac{3}{x} = \dfrac{6}{20}$

9) $\dfrac{x}{12} = \dfrac{2}{3}$

10) $\dfrac{7}{x} = \dfrac{7}{3}$

11) $\dfrac{5}{9} = \dfrac{10}{x}$

12) $\dfrac{6}{1} = \dfrac{6}{x}$

13) $\frac{8}{4} = \frac{x}{5}$

15) $\frac{9}{3} = \frac{x}{9}$

14) $\frac{7}{3} = \frac{28}{x}$

Set B

1) $\frac{5}{2} = \frac{10}{x}$

2) $\frac{6}{x} = \frac{3}{2}$

3) $\frac{x}{3} = \frac{15}{5}$

4) $\frac{25}{x} = \frac{40}{8}$

5) $\frac{x}{4} = \frac{4}{16}$

6) $\frac{28}{4} = \frac{x}{7}$

7) $\frac{3}{9} = \frac{9}{x}$

8) $\frac{6}{x} = \frac{15}{30}$

9) $\frac{x}{15} = \frac{4}{5}$

10) $\frac{8}{x} = \frac{8}{3}$

11) $\frac{3}{8} = \frac{6}{x}$

12) $\frac{7}{1} = \frac{7}{x}$

13) $\frac{10}{5} = \frac{x}{2}$

14) $\frac{9}{5} = \frac{19}{x}$

15) $\frac{12}{4} = \frac{x}{12}$

CONVERTING PERCENTAGES TO DECIMALS (DIVIDING BY 100)

In each of the following 15 problems, convert the percentage listed into the appropriate decimal.

Set A

1) 10%

2) 1%

3) 15%

4) 50%

5) 38%

6) 62%

7) 3%

8) 79%

9) 23%

10) 86.5%

11) 12.9%

12) 46.7%

13) 90.3%

14) 2.25%

15) 100%

Set B

1) 20%

2) 2%

3) 12%

4) 25%

5) 36%

6) 55%

7) 4%

8) 82%

9) 27%

10) 83.5%

11) 13.1%

12) 47.8%

13) 80.4%

14) 3.35%

15) 0%

EXPONENTS

In the following 15 problems, evaluate the given exponents. **Show all your work.**

Set A

1) 2^0

2) 2^1

3) 2^2

4) 3^1

5) 3^2

6) 2^3

7) 2^4

8) 3^3

9) 4^2

10) 5^2

11) 4^3

12) 5^3

13) 6^2

14) 8^3

15) 10^5

Set B

1) 1^0

2) 1^1

3) 1^2

4) 4^1

5) 4^2

6) 2^4

7) 2^5

8) 3^4

9) 7^2

10) 8^2

11) 3^3

12) 4^3

13) 9^2

14) 9^3

15) 10^4

DIVISIBILITY RULES

In the following problems, evaluate whether each number is divisible by the given number.

10. 94, 635

State whether the number is divisible by 2:

1. 53,764
2. 1,246
3. 69,749
4. 738
5. 9,350
6. 47
7. 2,182
8. 92
9. 345
10. 15

State whether the number is divisible by 3:

1. 1353
2. 36,696
3. 4,567
4. 35
5. 8,241
6. 56
7. 99
8. 789
9. 538
10. 3,578

State whether the number is divisible by 4:

1. 567
2. 360
3. 124
4. 15,671
5. 748
6. 991
7. 608
8. 4,364
9. 2,355

State whether the number is divisible by 6:

1. 4,728
2. 627
3. 72
4. 96
5. 374
6. 564
7. 1,745
8. 2,530
9. 5,844
10. 7,352

State whether the number is divisible by 7:

1. 91
2. 74
3. 99
4. 154
5. 280
6. 360
7. 999
8. 5,145
9. 3,581
10. 4, 263

State whether the number is divisible by 9:

1. 98
2. 877
3. 180
4. 207
5. 450
6. 551
7. 3,204

8. 6,780
9. 3,057

10. 56,981

LONG DIVISION

In the following 15 problems, evaluate the given expressions. All answers should be rounded to the nearest hundredth (.01). **Show all work in a neat and organized manner. Use extra paper if necessary.**

Set A

1) $19 \div 5$

2) $22 \div 4$

3) $36 \div 8$

4) $49 \div 6$

5) $64 \div 9$

6) $81 \div 7$

7) $100 \div 3$

8) $1 \div 3$

9) $1 \div 2$

10) $1 \div 4$

11) $1 \div 5$

12) $3 \div 5$

13) $3 \div 4$

14) $3 \div 8$

15) $4 \div 9$

Set B

1) $17 \div 4$

2) $21 \div 5$

3) $33 \div 9$

4) $48 \div 7$

5) $66 \div 8$

6) $80 \div 7$

7) $100 \div 6$

8) $1 \div 4$

9) $1 \div 7$

10) $1 \div 9$

11) $1 \div 10$

12) $2 \div 5$

13) $2 \div 6$

14) $4 \div 5$

15) $5 \div 9$

ORDER OF OPERATIONS

In the following 15 problems, evaluate the given expressions. Remember PEMDAS. Do long division if necessary, and round answers to the nearest hundredth (.01). **Show all work.**

Set A

1) $2 + 5 \times 3$

2) $(2 + 5) \times 3$

3) $5 + 2^2 \times 3$

4) $100 - 7^2 + 9 \div 3$

5) $100 - (7^2 + 2) \div 3$

6) $(100 - 7^2 + 9) \div 3$

7) $48 - 4 \times 2^3 \div 2 + 8$

8) $48 - 4 \times (2^3 \div 2 + 8)$

9) $(48 - 4 \times 2^3) \div 2 + 8$

10) $(48 - 4) \times 2^3 \div 2 + 8$

11) $48 - 4 \times 2^3 \div (2 + 8)$

12) $3 \times 16 - 4^2 + 8 \div 4$

13) $3 \times 16 - (4^2 + 8 \div 4)$

14) $3 \times (16 - 4^2 + 8) \div 4$

15) $3 \times (16 - 4^2) + 8 \div 4$

Set B

1) $3 + 6 \times 2$

2) $(3 + 6) \times 2$

3) $4 + 3^2 \times 2$

4) $90 - 6^2 + 10 \div 2$

5) $90 - (6^2 + 10) \div 2$

6) $(90 - 6^2 + 10) \div 2$

7) $52 - 2 \times 2^4 \div 4 + 2$

8) $52 - 2 \times (2^4 \div 4 + 2)$

9) $(52 - 2 \times 2^4) \div 4 + 2$

10) $(52 - 2) \times 2^4 \div 4 + 2$

11) $52 - 2 \times 2^4 \div (4 + 2)$

12) $4 \times 14 - 5^2 + 12 \div 3$

13) $4 \times 14 - (5^2 + 12 \div 3)$

14) $4 \times (14 - 5^2 + 12) \div 3$

15) $4 \times (14 - 5^2) + 12 \div 3$

RATIOS AND PROPORTIONS

In each of the following 15 problems involving ratios and proportions, follow the instructions closely to provide the information requested. All answers should be reduced if necessary. **Show all work in a neat and organized manner.**

Set A

Questions 1-3 refer to the following statement:

There are 4 lilies and 9 daffodils in the garden.

1) What is the ratio of lilies to daffodils?

2) What is the ratio of daffodils to total flowers in the garden?

3) What is the ratio of lilies to total flowers in the garden?

Questions 4-6 refer to the statement written below:

There are 28 tigers and 15 lions in the zoo.

4) What is the ratio of tigers to lions?

5) What is the ratio of tigers to the total number of tigers and lions in the zoo?

6) What is the ratio of lions to the total number of tigers and lions in the zoo?

7) The local vegetable seller buys 75 red peppers, 125 leeks and 60 carrots from the vendor. Find the ratio of the number of red peppers to the total amount of vegetables purchased.

8) The local fruit seller purchases 80 oranges, 140 pears and 30 guavas from the vendor. Find the ratio of oranges to pears.

9) Lucy has twelve marbles. Three are blue, four are red, two are green and the remaining ones are yellow. What is the ratio of blue marbles to green marbles?

In the following 3 problems (10-12), find the amounts requested based on the ratios given:

10) In Tribeca's local soccer league, the male to female ratio is 6:5. If there are 121 players in the league, how many male players are there? How many female players?

11) Nicholas has a record of winning 2 chess matches for every 3 he loses. If he had 65 matches during the last year, how many matches did he win? How many did he lose?

12) It is Frederick's first day of school. Having too much fun over the summer, he only bought three out of every five of the items required for the school year period. If there were 20 items assigned, how many items is he missing?

13) Four out of every seven puppies in a group of 84 German Shepherds have floppy ears. How many have *non*-floppy ears?

In the following 2 problems, find the ratios requested:

14) The old US nickel was made out of 2.4 grams of nickel and 3.2 grams of copper. Find the ratio of nickel to copper.

15) Professor Colburn's biology lecture contains 175 people. At the beginning of the semester she awards one-fifth of her students the opportunity to do outside research. Professor Stone's chemistry lecture contains 63 students. He offers the same research opportunity to his students, awarding only one-third this privilege. What will be the ratio of Colburn's winners to Stone's?

Set B

Questions 1-3 refer to the following statement:

There are 6 knives and 10 forks in the dishwasher.

1) What is the ratio of knives to forks?

2) What is the ratio of forks to total silverware in the dishwasher?

3) What is the ratio of knives to total silverware in the dishwasher?

Questions 4-6 refer to the following statement:

There are 12 puppies and 7 kittens at the veterinarian's office.

4) What is the ratio of puppies to kittens?

5) What is the ratio of puppies to the total number of puppies and kittens?

6) What is the ratio of kittens to the total number of puppies and kittens?

7) The local library purchases 50 books, 20 compact discs, and 40 videos to supplement its current collection. Find the ratio of the number of books to the total number of items purchased.

8) At the carnival, the balloon artist makes 55 dogs, 83 horses, and 105 elephants. Find the ratio of horses to elephants.

9) Fred has eighteen cards. Three are spades, four are hearts, six are clubs, and the remaining cards are diamonds. What is the ratio of hearts to diamonds?

In the following problems, find the amounts requested based on the ratios given:

10) In Tina's class, the ratio of boys to girls is 2:3. If there are 35 kids in the class, how many boys are there? How many girls?

11) School of the Future wins four soccer games for every three it loses. If the school played 56 games last season, how many did it win? How many did it lose?

12) Stacy can only find five grocery items for every seven on her shopping list. If there are 28 items on her list, how many is she unable to find?

13) Nine out of every 25 students in the fourth grade are only children. If there are 150 students in the fourth grade, how many *have siblings*?

In the following two problems, find the ratios requested:

14) Carlo's lemon cookies contain 1.8 grams of sodium for every 4.5 grams of sugar. Find the ratio of sodium to sugar.

15) There are 64 students in Professor Johnson's advanced chemistry class. One-eighth of them will drop out before the semester is over. Professor Anderson's class has 54 students. One-ninth of them will drop out. What will be the ratio of students who drop Johnson's class to those who drop Anderson's?

MATHEMATICAL VOCABULARY

In the following 15 problems, list examples of the numbers requested or answer the question as indicated.

1. Give one whole or natural number.

2. List two different numbers that are not whole or natural.

3. List three different numbers that are integers.

4. List four different numbers that are not integers.

5. List five different numbers that are composite.

6. List six different prime numbers.

7. List three different numbers that are rational.

8. Give one number that is irrational.

9. List two numbers that are real.

10. Give one number that is imaginary.

11. Give one number that is complex.

12. List two numbers that are both natural and prime.

13. List three numbers that are prime, but not natural numbers.

14. How many irrational numbers are also prime numbers?

15. How many numbers are both rational and complex?

SIGNIFICANCE OF 0 AND 1

In the following 15 problems, perform the operations indicated in the expressions.

Set A

1. $x \cdot 0$

2. $x \cdot 1$

3. $0 \div x$

4. $x \div 0$

5. $x \div 1$

6. x^0

7. x^1

8. $3z^2 \cdot 1$

9. $0 \cdot 6r^4$

10. $0 \div 8g^3$

11. $5m^5 \div 1$

12. 0^{9x}

13. 1^{7y}

14. $(4d^2)^1$

15. $(2p^{12})^0$

Set B

1. $0 \cdot y$

2. $1 \cdot y$

3. $y \div 1$

4. $y \div y$

5. 1^y

6. 0^y

7. $w^2 \cdot 0$

8. $4p^2 \cdot 1$

9. $0 \cdot (3a)^3$

10. $9q^4 \div 1$

11. $0(5x)^2$

12. $1(5y)^3$

13. $(7b^3)^1$

14. $(3u^{10})^0$

15. $((17n^8)^0)^1$

SHADED REGIONS AND NESTED FIGURES

In each of the following 15 problems, determine the areas requested. Be sure to include the appropriate units of measurement in your answers.

Use the figures below to answer questions 1-4. The area of each grid square shown is 3 cm^2.

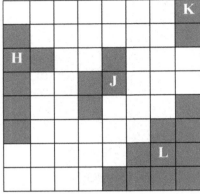

1. What is the area of figure L?

2. What is the difference between the areas of figure H and figure J?

3. What is the sum of the areas of figure J and figure K?

4. What is the product of the areas of figure H and figure L?

Use the figure below to answer questions 5-9. All measurements are in centimeters.

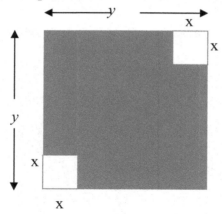

5. What is the area of the largest square?

6. What is the combined area of the two smaller squares?

7. What is the area of the shaded region?

8. What is the difference between the area of the shaded region and the combined area of the two smaller squares?

9. If y is equal to $4x$, what portion of the largest square is taken up by the smaller squares? Give your answer as a fraction and as a percentage.

Use the figure below to answer questions 10-15. The larger square has a side length of 10 ft, as shown. A circle is inscribed inside this square. A smaller square of side length *x*ft is inscribed inside the circle.

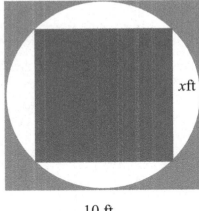

10 ft

10. What is the area of the larger square?

11. What is the area of the smaller square?

12. What is the difference between the area of the larger square and the area of the smaller square?

13. What is the diagonal of the smaller square?

14. What is the area of the portion of the circle that is not covered by the smaller square?

15. What is the area of the shaded portion of the entire figure?

COMBINATIONS AND PROBABILITY

For each of the following 15 problems, provide the information requested. Pay close attention to the form in which the answer is requested. Make sure that all answers are in their simplest forms.

Set A

1. Ramon has three favorite sweaters. He also has four favorite shirts. How many different combinations of Ramon's favorite sweaters and shirts are possible?

2. In addition to his favorite sweaters and his favorite shirts, Ramon also has two favorite pairs of socks. How many different combinations of Ramon's favorite sweaters, shirts, and socks are possible?

3. Of Ramon's three favorite sweaters, one is green, one is blue, and one is grey. What is the probability that the sweater Ramon chooses will be blue?

4. Of Ramon's four favorite shirts, two are white, one is blue, and one is brown. What is the probability that Ramon will choose a blue sweater and a blue shirt?

5. Of Ramon's two favorite pairs of socks, one is grey, and one is black. What is the probability that Ramon will choose a green sweater, a white shirt, and black socks?

For questions 6-10, use the information below.

Two cards are chosen at random, each one from a separate deck of cards. The table below shows some of the possible outcomes and the probability of each of those outcomes.

Number of Diamonds	Probability
0	9/16
1	3/8
2	1/16

Number of Spades	Probability
0	9/16
1	3/8
2	1/16

6. What is the probability that neither of the cards chosen will be a diamond or a spade? Give your answer both as a fraction and as a percentage.

7. What is the probability that there will be either two diamonds or two spades chosen?

8. What is the probability that there will be one diamond and one spade chosen? Give your answer both as a fraction and as a percentage.

9. What are the chances that neither of the cards chosen will be a diamond or a spade, compared to the chance that there will be one diamond and one spade?

10. What is the expected number of diamonds? What is the expected number of spades?

For questions 11-15, use the information below.

Chelsea has a bag of jelly beans. The bag contains 6 cherry, 3 orange, 6 raspberry, 8 apple, 3 lemon, and 4 blueberry jelly beans.

11. If Chelsea takes a jelly bean out randomly from the bag, what is the probability that it will be cherry?

12. If Chelsea takes a jelly bean out randomly from the bag, what is the probability that it will be orange, apple, or blueberry?

13. If Chelsea picks out 2 lemon jelly beans and eats them, and then picks out another jelly bean randomly from the bag, what is the probability that the jelly bean will be raspberry or lemon?

14. If Chelsea picks out 6 apple jelly beans and 4 raspberry jelly beans and eats them, and then picks out another jelly bean randomly from the bag, what is the probability that the jelly bean will be blueberry?

15. If Chelsea picks an apple jelly bean from the bag randomly and eats it, what is the probability that the next jelly bean she chooses is lemon? What is the probability that both things happen?

Set B

1.   Andrew has five pairs of socks and three pairs of shoes. How many different combinations of Andrew's socks and shoes are possible?

2.   If Andrew always wears one of two hats, how many different combinations of socks, shoes, and hats are possible?

3.   Of Andrew's five pairs of socks, one is black, one is beige, and the rest are white. What is the probability that the socks Andrew chooses will be white?

4.   Of Andrew's three pairs of shoes, one is black, one is brown, and one is white. What is the probability that Andrew will choose white socks and black shoes?

5.   Of Andrew's two hats, one is white and one is black. What is the probability that Andrew will choose white socks, brown shoes, and a black hat?

For questions 6-10, use the information below.

Two playing pieces are chosen at random from a board game. Each piece is either red, yellow, blue or green. The table below shows some of the possible outcomes and the probability of each of those outcomes.

Number of Red Pieces	Probability
0	$\dfrac{7}{10}$
1	$\dfrac{2}{5}$
2	$\dfrac{1}{20}$

Number of Blue Pieces	Probability
0	$\dfrac{7}{10}$
1	$\dfrac{2}{5}$
2	$\dfrac{1}{20}$

6.   What is the probability that neither of the pieces chosen will be red or blue? Give your answer both as a fraction and as a percentage.

7.   What is the probability that there will be one red piece and one blue piece chosen? Give your answer both as a fraction and as a percentage.

8. What is the probability that both pieces will be blue or that both pieces will be red?

9. What is the probability that there will be one red piece and no blue pieces chosen? Give your answer both as a fraction and as a percentage.

10.   What is the likelihood that there will be one red piece and no blue piece chosen, compared with the likelihood there will be one red piece and one blue piece?

For questions 11-15, use the information below.

Jenny has a bag of lollipops. The bag contains 4 lime, 7 orange, 5 grape, 6 blueberry, and 3 chocolate lollipops.

11.   If Jenny takes a lollipop out randomly from the bag, what is the probability that it will be lime?

12.   If Jenny takes a lollipop out randomly from the bag, what is the probability that it will be orange, blueberry, or chocolate?

13.   If Jenny takes a lollipop out randomly from the bag, what is the probability that it will NOT be orange or grape?

14.   If Jenny picks out two lollipops, what is the probability that the first one will be blueberry and the second one will be chocolate?

15.   Is it more likely that Jenny will pick out either a lime or grape lollipop, or is it more likely that she will pick out either a blueberry or chocolate lollipop?

MEAN, MEDIAN, AND MODE

In the following 15 problems, calculate the requested figures. Pay close attention to the distinction between mean, median, and mode.

Set A

1. Monty is a plumber who wants to calculate the mean of his daily earnings in one work week. From Monday to Thursday, he earned $500 for one job. On Friday, he worked a different job, for which he earned $100. What is the mean of his daily earnings from Monday to Friday?

2. Monty is now curious about the mode of his daily earnings. Assuming Monty earned the same amount of money on each day of the four-day job, what is the mode of his daily earnings from Monday to Friday?

3. Finally, Monty would like to figure out the median of his daily earnings. Assuming Monty earned the same amount of money on each day of the four-day job, what is the median of his daily earnings from Monday to Friday?

Use the information below for questions 4-7. Jamie made a chart that shows the number of countries that each of her eight closest friends has visited.

Friend	Number of Countries
Alison	3
Barry	1
Claire	9
David	2
Emily	4
Frank	2
Georgia	2
Horace	5

Statistical Measure	Value
Mean	?
Median	?
Mode	?
Range	?

4. Fill in Jamie's statistical measure chart.

5. If the number of countries that each of Jamie's friends has visited were increased by 4, which one of the statistical measures would change the least?

6. If the number of countries that each of Jamie's friends has visited were multiplied by 4, which of the statistical measures would change the most? Which would change the least?

7. If the number of countries that each of Jamie's friends has visited were squared, which of the statistical measures would change the most? Which would change the least?

Use the information below for questions 8-11.

Mr. Feldman offered a retest to five students who were sick on the day of his exam. Below is a chart detailing the scores.

Student	Score
Vikram	81
Wendy	92
Xavier	?
Yolanda	94
Zeke	?

8. If the mean of the five scores is 85, what is the mean of Xavier and Zeke's scores?

9. If Zeke's score is the same as the mean of the five scores, what is Xavier's score?

10. Xavier has asked for some extra credit on his exam. How many extra points would he need in order to bring the mean of the five scores up to 87? What score would that give him?

11. If Mr. Feldman decided to curve the exam scores and give every student an equal number of extra points, how many points would each student need in order to bring the mean of the five scores up to 88?

Use the information below for questions 12-15.

The student body of Glendale High is between the ages of 14 and 18. The graph below shows the number of students by age.

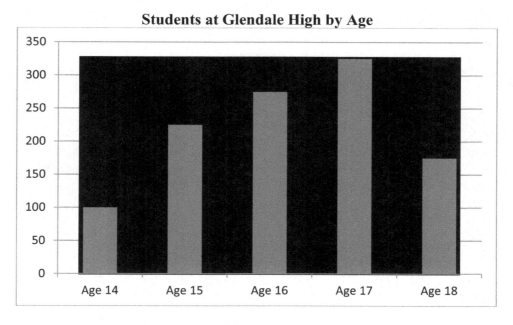

12. What is the total population of the Glendale High student body?

13. What is the mode of the set of data?

14. What is the median of the set of data?

15. What is the mean of the set of data? Round your answer to the nearest hundredth.

Set B

1.   Stan goes on a 10-day vacation. The first five days, he spends $1200 on a cruise. In the remaining five days, he spends $450 on a round-trip flight to San Francisco, where he spends $300 on food and entertainment. (He does not need a hotel room because he stays with friends.) What is the mean of Stan's daily expenses for the 10 days of his vacation?

2.   Stan's friend, Alex, joins him on part of the vacation. Alex spends $37, $41, $50, $41, and $34 on the five days that he and Stan are in San Francisco. What is the mode of Alex's daily expenses?

3.   What is the median of Alex's daily expenses during the five days he and Stan are in San Francisco?

Use the information below for questions 4-7.

Denise made a chart that shows the number of states that each of her six closest friends has visited.

Friend	Number of States
Abby	12
Blake	22
Connor	4
Danielle	2
Eddie	14
Fiona	12

Statistical Measure	Value
Mean	?
Median	?
Mode	?
Range	?

4.   Fill in Denise's statistical measure chart.

5.   If the number of states that each of Denise's friends has visited were increased by 5, which of the statistical measures would change the least?

6.   If the number of states that each of Denise's friends has visited were multiplied by 2, which of the statistical measures would change the most? Which one would change the least?

7.   If the number of states that each of Denise's friends had been to were divided by two, which of the statistical measures would change the most? Which would change the least?

Use the information below for questions 8-11.

The school nurse took the temperature of four students who were not feeling well on Tuesday. Below is a chart detailing the temperatures.

Student	Temp.
Will	99.4
Xena	101
Yael	?
Zoey	99.6

8. If the mean of the four temperatures was 100, what was Yael's temperature?

9. If the temperature of a fifth student – Victor – was also taken and turned out to be normal (98.6), what would the mean temperature of the five students be?

10. Xena's mom is going to pick her up early unless her temperature is back to normal (98.6) by 12:30. How many degrees lower would the mean temperature of the original four students drop if Xena's did come down to normal?

11. If Will's temperature is up to 100.1 by lunch time while Xena's and Yael's remain constant, what must Zoey's temperature be for the means NOT to change?

Use the information below to answer questions 12-15.

There are five teams in the Eastwick Basketball League. Their average point totals per game over the course of the season are listed below.

Team	Avg. Point Total
Panthers	56
Tigers	72
Badgers	37
Penguins	49
Bears	85

12.   What is the mean number of points scored per game for all five teams in the league?

13.   What is the difference between the median of the above point totals and the range of the above point totals?

14. If the Panthers' average point total increased by 50%, how would the mean number of points scored per game change for all five teams in the league?

15. If the Penguins' average point total decreased by 16 points and the Badgers' average point total increased by 18 points, how would the median number of points scored per game change for all five teams in the league?

ABSOLUTE VALUE

In the following 15 problems, calculate the value(s) of x based on the information given.

Set A

1. What are the possible values of x if $|x| = 7$?

2. What are the possible values of x if $|x + 2| = 7$?

3. What is the set of possible values of x if $|x + 2| > 7$?

       Draw this set on a number line.

4. What is the set of possible values of x if $|x + 2| \leq 7$?

       Draw this set on a number line.

5. What are the possible values of x if $|2x| = 14$?

6. What are the possible values of x if $|2x - 4| = 14$?

7. What is the set of possible values of x if $|2x - 4| < 14$?

Draw this set on a number line.

8. What is the set of possible values of x if $|2x - 4| \geq 14$?

Draw this set on a number line.

9. What are the possible values of x if $|x + 16| = 9$?

10. What are the possible values of x if $|2x + 10| = 4$?

11. What is the set of possible values of x if $|2x + 10| < 4$?

12. What is the set of possible values of x if $|2x + 10| > 4$?

13. What are the possible values of x if $|x + 6| = 2x + 4$?

14. What are the possible values of x if $|x - 5| = 3x - 11$?

15. What is the set of possible values of x if $|x - 5| < 3x - 11$?

Set B

1. What are the possible values of x if $|x| = 9$?

2. What are the possible values of x if $|x - 3| = 9$?

3. What is the set of possible values of x if $|x - 3| > 9$?

4. What is the set of possible values of x if $|x - 3| \leq 9$?

5. What are the possible values of x if $|3x| = 18$?

6. What are the possible values of x if $|3x + 9| = 12$?

7. What is the set of possible values of x if $|3x - 7| < 12$?

8. What is the set of possible values of x if $|3x + 9| \geq 12$?

9. What are the possible values of x if $|5x + 12| = 7$?

10. What is the set of possible values of x if $|5x + 12| = 7x$?

11. What is the set of possible values of x if $|5x + 12| \geq 7x$?

12. What are the possible values of x if $|x + 15| = 6$ and $|x - 6| = 27$?

13. What are the possible values of x if $|x + 4| = 2x + 4$?

14. What are the possible values of x if $|x + 4| = x + 4$?

15. What is the set of possible values of x if $|x + 4| \leq 2x + 4$?

OPERATIONS WITH EXPONENTS

In the following 15 problems, perform the operations in each expression.

Set A

1. $x^2 \cdot x^3$

2. $x^4 \cdot x^5$

3. $x^3 \div x^2$

4. $x^8 \div x^5$

5. $3x^2 \cdot 12x^3$

6. $12x^3 \div 3x^2$

7. $9x^3 \cdot 15x^4$

8. $20x^7 \div 4x^5$

9. $(x^3)^2$

10. $(x^4)^3$

11. $(2x^3)^2$

12. $(5x^4)^3$

13. $\sqrt{(x^6)}$

14. $\sqrt{(4x^8)}$

15. $\sqrt{(36x^{10})}$

Set B

1. $x \cdot x^2$

8. $27x^6 \div 9x^2$

2. $x^3 \cdot x^5$

9. $(x^4)^2$

10. $(x^5)^3$

3. $x^4 \div x$

11. $(3x^5)^2$

4. $x^9 \div x^3$

12. $(4x^3)^3$

5. $2x^3 \cdot 10x^4$

13. $\sqrt{(x^8)}$

6. $16x^5 \div 4x^2$

14. $\sqrt{(9x^6)}$

7. $8x^5 \cdot 11x^4$

15. $\sqrt{(49x^{12})}$

MATH WORKSHEETS ANSWER KEY

Addition and Subtraction of Fractions

Set A

1. 1

2. $\frac{2}{3}$

3. $\frac{1}{2}$

4. $\frac{1}{3}$

5. $\frac{1}{2}$

6. $\frac{2}{3}$

7. $\frac{3}{4}$

8. $\frac{1}{2}$

9. $\frac{5}{6}$

10. $\frac{5}{12}$

11. $\frac{5}{12}$

12. $\frac{19}{24}$

13. $\frac{43}{56}$

14. $\frac{17}{45}$

15. $\frac{1}{30}$

Set B

1. 1

2. $\frac{2}{3}$

3. $\frac{4}{5}$

4. $\frac{2}{9}$

5. $\frac{3}{8}$

6. $\frac{1}{2}$

7. $\frac{5}{8}$

8. $\frac{4}{9}$

9. $\frac{5}{12}$

10. $\frac{1}{4}$

11. $\frac{7}{15}$

12. $\frac{23}{24}$

13. $\frac{13}{18}$

14. $\frac{11}{40}$

15. $\frac{19}{56}$

Multiplication and Division of Fractions

Set A

1. $\frac{1}{4}$

2. $\frac{1}{9}$

3. $\frac{1}{16}$

4. 2

5. 3

6. 5

7. $\frac{1}{8}$

8. $\frac{1}{18}$

9. $\frac{2}{3}$

10. $\frac{2}{3}$

11. $\frac{3}{8}$

12. $\frac{1}{4}$

13. $\frac{24}{25}$

14. $\frac{5}{56}$

15. $\frac{18}{35}$

Set B

1. $\frac{1}{25}$

2. $\frac{1}{36}$

3. $\frac{4}{9}$

4. 2

5. 2

6. $\frac{7}{2}$

7. $\frac{1}{16}$

8. $\frac{1}{27}$

9. $\frac{1}{24}$

10. $\frac{3}{2}$

11. $\frac{12}{5}$

12. $\frac{5}{24}$

13. $\frac{10}{3}$

14. $\frac{21}{40}$

15. $\frac{40}{21}$

Converting an Improper Fraction to a Mixed Fraction

Set A

1. $1\frac{1}{2}$

2. $2\frac{1}{3}$

3. $2\frac{2}{5}$

4. $2\frac{1}{4}$

5. $1\frac{2}{3}$

6. 4

7. $5\frac{3}{7}$

8. $2\frac{1}{2}$

9. $4\frac{1}{2}$

10. $2\frac{2}{9}$

11. $2\frac{1}{4}$

12. $3\frac{2}{3}$

13. $11\frac{1}{5}$

14. $9\frac{1}{11}$

15. $10\frac{1}{25}$

Set B

1. $1\frac{1}{4}$

2. $3\frac{1}{2}$

3. $2\frac{1}{4}$

4. $3\frac{1}{3}$

5. $1\frac{3}{5}$

6. 3

7. $6\frac{1}{4}$

8. $4\frac{1}{2}$

9. $4\frac{1}{10}$

10. $2\frac{3}{4}$

11. $2\frac{1}{11}$

12. $2\frac{5}{7}$

13. $8\frac{1}{6}$

14. $10\frac{2}{3}$

15. $7\frac{1}{52}$

Converting a Mixed Fraction to an Improper Fraction

Set A

1. $\frac{3}{2}$

2. $\frac{10}{3}$

3. $\frac{25}{6}$

4. $\frac{8}{5}$

5. $\frac{21}{8}$

6. $\frac{25}{7}$

7. $\frac{35}{4}$

8. $\frac{91}{9}$

9. $\frac{39}{16}$

10. $\frac{59}{12}$

11. $\frac{41}{6}$

12. $\frac{38}{3}$

13. $\frac{63}{4}$

14. $\frac{113}{12}$

15. $\frac{161}{9}$

Set B

1. $\frac{4}{3}$

2. $\frac{5}{2}$

3. $\frac{13}{4}$

4. $\frac{13}{8}$

5. $\frac{27}{8}$

6. $\frac{39}{8}$

7. $\frac{29}{3}$

8. $\frac{73}{6}$

9. $\frac{37}{14}$

10. $\frac{59}{15}$

11. $\frac{63}{8}$

12. $\frac{59}{4}$

13. $\frac{56}{3}$

14. $\frac{103}{12}$

15. $\frac{139}{10}$

Algebra

Set A

1. 2
2. 4
3. 6
4. 7
5. 12
6. 2
7. 5
8. 4
9. 3
10. 1
11. 2
12. 3
13. 2
14. 8
15. 9

Set B

1. $x = 2$
2. $y = 10$
3. $z = 6$
4. $a = 7$
5. $b = 11$
6. $c = 3$
7. $x = 2$
8. $y = 5$
9. $b = 4$
10. $z = 3$
11. $x = 5$
12. $p = 6$
13. $z = 2$
14. $b = 8$
15. $c = 10$

Cross Multiplication

Set A

1. 3
2. 28
3. 10
4. 40
5. 1
6. 9
7. 32
8. 10
9. 8
10. 3
11. 18
12. 1
13. 10
14. 12
15. 27

Set B

1. $x = 4$
2. $x = 4$
3. $x = 9$
4. $x = 5$
5. $x = 1$
6. $x = 49$
7. $x = 27$
8. $x = 12$
9. $x = 12$
10. $x = 3$
11. $x = 16$
12. $x = 1$
13. $x = 4$
14. $x = 10.56$
15. $x = 36$

Converting Percentages to Decimals (Dividing by 100)

Set A

1. 0.1
2. 0.01
3. 0.15
4. 0.5
5. 0.38
6. 0.62
7. 0.03
8. 0.79
9. 0.23
10. 0.865
11. 0.129
12. 0.467
13. 0.903
14. 0.0225
15. 1

Set B

1. 0.2
2. 0.02
3. 0.12
4. 0.25
5. 0.36
6. 0.55
7. 0.04
8. 0.82
9. 0.27
10. 0.835
11. 0.131
12. 0.478
13. 0.804
14. 0.0335
15. 0

Exponents

Set A

1. 1
2. 2
3. 4
4. 3
5. 9
6. 8
7. 16
8. 27
9. 16
10. 25
11. 64
12. 125
13. 36
14. 512
15. 100,000

Set B

1. 1
2. 1
3. 1
4. 4
5. 16
6. 16
7. 32
8. 81
9. 49
10. 64
11. 27
12. 64
13. 81
14. 81
15. 10,000

Divisibility

State whether the number is divisible by 2.

1. 53,764 - divisible
2. 1,246 - divisible
3. 69,749 - not divisible
4. 738 - divisible
5. 9,350 - divisible
6. 47 - not divisible
7. 2,182 - divisible
8. 92 - divisible
9. 345 - not divisible
10. 15 - not divisible

State whether the number is divisible by 3.

1. 1,353 - divisible
2. 36,696 - divisible
3. 4,567 - not divisible
4. 35 - not divisible
5. 8,241 - divisible
6. 56 - not divisible
7. 99 - divisible
8. 789 - divisible
9. 538 - not divisible
10. 3,578 - not divisible

State whether the number is divisible by 4.

1. 567 - not divisible
2. 360 - divisible
3. 124 - divisible
4. 15,671 - not divisible
5. 748 - divisible
6. 991 - not divisible
7. 608 - divisible
8. 4,364 - divisible
9. 2,355 - divisible
10. 94,635 - not divisible

State whether the number is divisible by 6.

1. 4,728 - divisible
2. 627 - not divisible
3. 72 - divisible

4. 96 - divisible
5. 374 - not divisible
6. 564 - divisible
7. 1,745 - not divisible
8. 2,530 - not divisible
9. 5,844 - divisible
10. 7,352 - not divisible

State whether the number is divisible by 7.

1. 91 - divisible
2. 74 - no divisible
3. 99 - not divisible
4. 154 - not divisible
5. 280 - divisible
6. 350 - divisible
7. 999 not divisible
8. 5,145 - divisible
9. 3,581 - not divisible
10. 4,263 - divisible

State whether the number is divisible by 9.

1. 98 - not divisible
2. 877- not divisible
3. 180 - divisible
4. 551 - not divisible
5. 207 - divisible
6. 450 - divisible
7. 3,204 - divisible
8. 6,780 - not divisible
9. 3,057 - not divisible
10. 56,981 - not divisible

Long Division

Set A

1. 3.80
2. 5.50
3. 4.50
4. 8.17
5. 7.11
6. 11.57
7. 33.33
8. 0.33
9. 0.50
10. 0.25
11. 0.20
12. 0.60
13. 0.75
14. 0.38
15. 0.44

Set B

1. 4.25
2. 4.2
3. 3.67
4. 6.86
5. 8.25
6. 11.43
7. 16.67
8. 0.25
9. 0.14
10. 0.11
11. 0.1
12. 0.4
13. 0.33
14. 0.8
15. 0.56

Order of Operations

Set A

1. 17
2. 21
3. 17
4. 54
5. 83
6. 20
7. 40
8. 0
9. 16
10. 184
11. 44.8
12. 34
13. 30
14. 6
15. 2

Set B

1. 15
2. 18
3. 22
4. 59
5. 22
6. 32
7. 46
8. 40
9. 7
10. 202
11. 46.67
12. 35
13. 37
14. 1.33
15. -40

Ratios and Proportions

Set A

1. 4:9
2. 9:13
3. 4:13
4. 28:15
5. 28:43
6. 15:43
7. 15:52
8. 4:7
9. 3:2
10. 66 male, 55 female
11. 26 won, 39 lost
12. 8 missing
13. 36
14. 3:4
15. 5:3

Set B

1. 3:5
2. 5:8
3. 3:8
4. 12:7
5. 12:19
6. 7:19
7. 5:11
8. 83:105
9. 4:5
10. 14 boys and 21 girls
11. 32 wins, 24 losses
12. 8
13. 96
14. 2:5
15. 4:3

Mathematical Vocabulary

1. Answers will vary
2. Answers will vary
3. Answers will vary
4. Answers will vary
5. Answers will vary
6. Answers will vary
7. Answers will vary
8. Answers will vary
9. Answers will vary
10. Answers will vary
11. Answers will vary
12. Answers will vary
13. Answers will vary
14. None
15. None

Significance of 0 and 1

Set A

1. 0
2. x
3. 0
4. Undefined
5. x
6. 1
7. x
8. $3z^2$
9. 0
10. 0
11. $5m^5$
12. 0
13. 1
14. $4d^2$
15. 1

Set B

1. 0
2. y
3. y
4. 1
5. 1
6. 0
7. 0
8. $4p^2$
9. 0
10. $9q^4$
11. 0
12. 1
13. $7b^3$
14. 1
15. 1

Shaded Regions and Nested Figures

1. 30 cm^2
2. 6 cm^2
3. 18 cm^2
4. 540 cm^2
5. y^2 cm^2
6. $2x^2$ cm^2
7. $y^2 - 2x^2$ cm^2
8. $y^2 - 4x^2$ cm^2
9. $\frac{1}{8}$, 12.5%
10. 100 ft^2
11. x^2 ft^2
12. $100 - x^2$ ft^2
13. $x\sqrt{2}$
14. $25\pi - x^2$ ft^2
15. $100 - 25\pi + x^2$ cm^2

Combinations and Probability

Set A

1. 12

2. 24

3. $\frac{1}{3}$

4. $\frac{1}{12}$

5. $\frac{1}{12}$

6. $\frac{81}{256}$, 32%

7. $\frac{1}{8}$

8. $\frac{9}{64}$, 14%

9. 18%

10. $\frac{1}{2}$

11. $\frac{1}{5}$

12. $\frac{1}{2}$

13. $\frac{1}{4}$

14. $\frac{1}{5}$

15. $\frac{4}{145}$

Set B

1. 15

2. 30

3. $\frac{3}{5}$

4. $\frac{1}{5}$

5. $\frac{1}{10}$

6. 49%

7. 16%

8. $\frac{1}{10}$

9. $\frac{7}{25}$ 28%

10. $\frac{3}{25}$

11. $\frac{4}{25}$

12. $\frac{16}{25}$

13. $\frac{13}{25}$

14. $\frac{3}{100}$

15. It is equally likely.

Mean, Median, and Mode

Set A

1. $120
2. $125
3. $125
4. Mean: 3.5; Median: 3; Mode: 2; Range: 8
5. Range
6. Range; Mode
7. Range; Mode
8. 79
9. 73
10. 10 extra points; 83
11. 1 point
12. 1,100
13. 17
14. 16
15. 16.23

Set B

1. $195
2. $41
3. $41
4. Mean: 11; Median: 13; Mode 12; Range: 20
5. Range
6. Range; Mean
7. Range; Mean
8. 100°
9. 99.7°
10. .6°
11. 98.9°
12. 59.8 points
13. 8 points
14. 65.4 points
15. 56 points

Absolute Value

Set A

1. 7, -7
2. 5, -9
3. $5 < x$ or $x < -9$
4. $-9 \leq x \leq 5$
5. 7, -7
6. 9, -5
7. $-5 < x < 9$
8. $x \leq -5$ or $x \geq 9$
9. -7, -25
10. $x = -3$, $x = -7$
11. $-7 < x < -3$
12. $x \leq -7$ or $x \geq -3$
13. $x = 2$, $x = -10/3$
14. $x = 3$, $x = 4$
15. $x \geq 4$

Set B

1. 9, -9
2. 12, -6
3. $x > 12$ or $x < -6$
4. $-6 \leq x \leq 12$
5. 6, -6
6. 1, -7
7. $-7 < x < 1$
8. $x \geq 1$ or $x \leq -7$
9. -1, -19/5
10. $x = 6$, $x = -1$
11. $6 \geq x$ or $x \leq -1$
12. -21
13. $x = 0$, $x = -8/3$
14. All numbers
15. $0 \leq x$ or $x \geq -8/3$

Operations with Exponents

Set A

1. x^5
2. x^9
3. x
4. x^3
5. $36x^5$
6. $4x$
7. $135x^7$
8. $5x^2$
9. x^6
10. x^{12}
11. $4x^6$
12. $125x^{12}$
13. x^3
14. $2x^4$
15. $6x^5$

Set B

1. x^3
2. x^8
3. x^3
4. x^6
5. $20x^7$
6. $4x^3$
7. $88x^9$
8. $3x^4$
9. x^8
10. x^{15}
11. $9x^{10}$
12. $64x^9$
13. x^4
14. $3x^3$
15. $7x^6$

Reading Comprehension

When possible, students should always read the entire passage before moving on to answer the questions, although skimming may also help is a student is having trouble with timing.

Remember that the answers to all questions should be coming directly from the passages themselves. Only in the case of inference questions will you be expected to make any sort of assumption without direct evidence.

Question Types

Main Idea

Most of the time, the first question on a passage will be about the main idea or primary purpose. Consider the overall passage and decide on its true focus.

Vocab-in-Context

These questions single out individual words within passages that may be of a higher level or have multiple meanings. Use the context in the sentence containing the word to determine its appropriate usage.

Specific Detail

These questions force students to recall individual facts from the passage. Use text support to answer these questions.

Inference

Inference questions are the only ones where the answers will not come out of direct evidence from the passage. Still, try to pinpoint a section of the passage that informs the inference.

Tone

These questions ask students to determine the prevailing mood or attitude of a passage. Look for words that indicate emotions in the passage.

Structural Purpose

Structural purpose questions less common than the other categories. These questions ask you to identify *why* an author chose to include a sentence or paragraph.

Tactics

Anticipate Answers

Before even reading the answer choices given, students should try to produce an independent response to each question. The anticipated answer does not need to be perfect in order to be useful.

Margin Notes

Many students do well when they annotate the passage. Try to make one note per paragraph, like a few words that label the main idea of that paragraph.

Underlining

This technique can work instead of margin notes to underline the key ideas and words. Underlining can help students stay focused on the passage.

Crossing Out

Cross out incorrect answers so that you are choosing from a smaller set of answers.

Numbering Proof

If you have a difficult time remembering to get your answers directly from the passage, try marking the point in the passage where you found each answer with the corresponding question number.

Add Up Your Margin Notes

It can be difficult to find evidence in a passage for main idea or primary purpose questions. Try considering the collection of margin notes that you've written for a given passage and see what it adds up to. If margin notes are done carefully, they should lead you to the main idea.

Tone = Emotion

Tone really amounts to emotion. Consider the passage and try to associate it with some emotion before matching it up against the options presented. At the very least, try to categorize your anticipated answer as positive, negative, or neutral.

The Missing Link

To understand the structure of a passage, look for transition words that connect topics and develop arguments (for example, "however" and "accordingly").

Questions First (optional)

Try reading the questions (but *not* the answer choices) about a passage before diving into the passage itself. This can clue you in to important sections on the first pass-through. In order to leave your mind open, avoid reading the answer choices until *after* you have anticipated the answer on your own.

This works well for some, but not all, students. Try it out to decide whether to read the passage or questions first.

The following page shows an example of a passage that has been analyzed using the strategies.

ISEE Reading Questions Analysis

Why Brooklyn Bridge is impressive

Q5d.
The Brooklyn Bride in New York has been featured in movies, photographs, and media for over a hundred years, but the bridge is much more than just a pretty sight. It opened on May 24, 1883, and, at 3,460 feet, it was the longest suspension bridge in the world, measuring 50% longer than any previously built. The Brooklyn Bridge was a symbol of American strength and vitality, but it's completion followed years of toil and sacrifice. ← *was a symbol* Q5a.

Begin. Problems Lots of them...

John Augustus Roebling, a German immigrant, envisioned the bridge that would link Manhattan to Brooklyn over the East River. While in preparations for building, however, John Roebling was injured when a ferry pinned his foot to a pylon, and he died weeks later of tetanus. Q3 This first setback to the building of the bridge was indicative of the problems that would plague its construction as well as the harrowing tenacity that led to its completion.

Son takes over, more problems

Washington Roebling took over the project upon his father's death. Washington persevered through many hurdles in the building of the bridge including fires, accidents, industrial Q2 corruption, and loss of public support. He continued, however, in his push to complete the bridge. In fact, it is said that he worked harder and longer than any worker he employed in even the most dangerous circumstances. While working in the caissons, underwater chambers that supported the bridge, he was stricken by the decompression sickness that led to his paralysis. Nothing could stop him, though, and he continued construction by sending messages to the site through his wife, Emily.

Bridge complete

Fourteen years after construction began, the Brooklyn Bridge celebrated its grand opening. The total cost to build the bridge was fifteen million dollars, and 27 people died in its construction, but it stood as a tribute to American invention and industry. ↓ Q5b.

1. The primary purpose of the passage is to?
(A) convince the reader that the Brooklyn Bridge is the longest suspension bridge in the world
(B) describe Washington Roebling's rise to success
(C) show that Americans have an inborn talent for inventiveness   *Add up margin notes*
(D) describe how the Brooklyn Bridge was a great success despite the hardships faced in building it

2. It can be inferred from the thirst paragraph that Washington Roebling
(A) was injured by a ferry   NO- dad was
(B) was determined to build the bridge despite many set backs   *numbering proof*
(C) suffered from depression after his injury   depression ≠ decompression
(D) had a son who completed the building of the bridge   NO - he was the son

3. Which one of the following is given as a difficulty faced in building the Brooklyn Bridge?
(A) an excessive number of pylons in the East River
(B) An outbreak of tetanus among the workers
(C) the death of the man who envisioned the bridge   *numbering proof*
(D) a lack of funds to keep building

4. Washington Roebling can best be described as
(A) persistent +
(B) weak —
(C) clumsy —   son who finished the bridge
(D) dangerous

5. Which of the following is NOT stated about the Brooklyn Bridge
(A) It was a sign of American power   Line 5
(B) It cost millions of dollars to build   Line 20
(C) it was not worth the money lost in building it   *numbering proof*
(D) It has been seen in the movies   Line 1

Remember that everyone is different, so some strategies may not work for everyone. Try out different combinations of the strategies to find what works best for each individual student.

IMPLEMENTING A SYSTEM FOR THE READING SECTION

Step 1: Read the questions (and **only** the questions):
- Keep in mind the information required to answer the questions as you read the passage

Step 2: Read the passage:
- Take margin notes
- Underline

Step 3: Re-read the question

Step 4: Identify the question type:
- Main idea
- Vocab-in-context
- Specific detail
- Inference
- Tone
- Structural purpose

Step 5: Apply the appropriate strategy:
- Add up your margin notes for main idea questions.
- Number proof for vocab-in-context, specific detail, inference, tone, and structural purpose questions.
- Tone = emotion for tone questions

Step 6: Anticipate an answer
- After applying the required strategy or strategies, create in your own words what you consider to be a satisfying answer.

Step 7: Eliminate unlikely options
- Using the anticipated answer as a guide, eliminate answer choices that seem to be way off, physically crossing them out.

Step 8: Select an Answer

Rhetorical Devices

Rhetorical devices are writing tools that authors can employ to entice readers.

Rhetorical Device Bank		
Device	**Meaning**	**Example**
Alliteration	the repetition of initial consonant sounds	*Falling fast, fleeting fancies*
Allusion	an indirect reference to an event, piece of literature, or person	*When faced with the opportunity to give, he was a Scrooge.*
Anaphora	beginning several lines with the same introductory phrase	Martin Luther King's "I Have a Dream" speech
Analogy	comparison of two things with similar characteristics	*I gazed at the buffet as a prisoner gazes at the sun-filled forest.*
Antithesis	opposing or contrasting ideas next to one another	*The further they got, the closer they became.*
Simile	comparison of two things using "like" or "as"	*The novel read like an instruction manual.*
Metaphor	implied comparison of two things	*His eyes were doors to another universe.*
Assonance	repetition of vowel sounds in non-rhyming words	*Go slowly over the road.*
Hyperbole	extreme exaggeration	*Her temper was apocalyptic.*
Onomatopoeia	words that sound like what they describe	*Hiss*
Oxymoron	a two-word paradox	*Jumbo shrimp*
Parallelism	using words or phrases with a similar structure	*It will not suffice to look back, nor to squabble, nor to make lofty plans.*

Personification	giving human qualities to nonhuman things	*The sun smiled.*
Rhetorical questions	a question that is asked to make a point, rather than to receive an answer.	*When the government refuses to intervene, who will?*
Repetition	repeated use of the same word or phrase to emphasize a point	*What will be will be.*
Understatement	deliberately describing something as less important than it really is	*With his beach vacation coming up, the climate crisis could wait.*
Ethos	persuading by appealing to ethics	Arguing for gender equality by saying that it is *right* to fight for gender equality
Logos	persuading by appealing to logic	Arguing for gender equality by saying it will improve overall work performance
Pathos	persuading by appealing to emotion	Arguing for gender equality by telling a harrowing story of one woman's suffering due to gender inequality

Verbal

The degree of emphasis on vocabulary varies across many secondary school admissions exams. However, each test touches on it in some way. Some tests, such as the ISEE and SSAT, involve vocabulary to a much greater extent than others. For these, it is critical for students to begin as early as possible to expand their vocabulary.

Student Strategies

Anticipate Answers
Before even reading the answer choices given, try to produce an independent response to each question.

Crossing Out
Cross out answers that do match the definition you anticipated. This is a visible reminder that from the initial options, only a more limited field will remain.

Word Roots
When faced with unfamiliar vocabulary, students should consider whether there are any morphemes (roots) that may help them decode meaning. Be careful of false roots that may trick students.

Context/Substitution
In sentence completion questions, try to identify the portion of each sentence that indicates what word should fit in the blank space. If possible, choose a word of your own that would fit the meaning of the sentence and match it to the answer choices.

Word Bridges
In analogy questions, it is far more concrete for students to replace the colon or the "is to" with a more descriptive phrase summarizing the relationship. For example, when given the analogy "bunny is to rabbit as...," it is helpful to re-imagine the statement as "bunny is a young rabbit as...." Look for an answer choice that fits the same "word bridge."

Draw it Out
*COOP/HSPT/TACHS: These tests contain logic questions. Try to uncover the solution to a problem through any possible visual method: charts, diagrams, etc. Think of logical reasoning sections as a combination of mathematical, reading comprehension, and verbal sections, as they draw on skills from each of these areas.

IMPLEMENTING A SYSTEM FOR THE VERBAL SECTION

Synonyms

Step 1: Read the question (and **only** the question)

Step 2: Ask "Do I know this word?"
- If yes, move on to step 3.
- If no, skip the question for now and return to it later if you have time.

Step 3: Anticipate an answer:
- Based on your knowledge of the word, decide what you consider to be its closest synonym.

Step 4: Eliminate unlikely options:
- Using the anticipated answer as a guide, eliminate answer choices that seem to be way off, physically crossing them out.

Step 5: Select an Answer

Sentence Completion

Step 1: Read the question (and **only** the question).

Step 2: Anticipate an answer:
- Based on the context of the sentence, create an option of your own that you think would fill the gap well.

Step 3: Eliminate unlikely options
- Using the anticipated answer as a guide, eliminate answer choices that seem to be way off, physically crossing them out.

Step 4: Select an Answer.

Breaking Down Vocabulary Words

Many words in the English language are made up of word parts called prefixes, roots, and suffixes. These word parts have specific meanings that, when added together, can help you determine the meaning of the word as a whole. Knowing the meanings of the most common word parts helps build an understanding for hundreds of words in the English language.

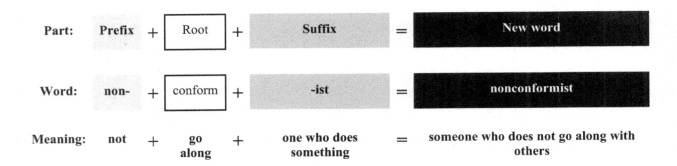

Prefixes

A prefix is a syllable, or group of syllables, added to the beginning of a word to alter its meaning. Prefixes help to add complexity to the English language by making it possible to create new words that are easily understood by speakers everywhere. Understanding a few prefix examples will help you to apply logic to the decoding of new words. Keep in mind, several prefixes serve to make the new word mean the opposite, or nearly the opposite, of the original meaning of the base word.

Word Root

Word roots are the words from other languages that are the origin of many English words. About 60% of all English words have Latin or Greek origins. Roots give words their fixed meaning. Prefixes and suffixes can then be attached to the roots to form new words.

Base Word

Base Words are words that can stand alone in English. These words have meaning on their own, but they can also have prefixes and suffixes added to them to make new words.

> For example: *cycle* is a full word in English, but it can also be added to, to make words like *bicycle* and *cyclist*. *Cycle* is the base word, or the simplest form of the word without any prefixes or suffixes.

Suffixes

Suffixes are a letter or group of letters added to the ending of words to change their meaning or function. These useful, shapeshifting tools can be as small as -s and -ed, or can be larger additions such as -ation and -ious.

Word Breakdown: Elements to Keep in Mind

- In most cases, a word is built upon at least one root.

- Words can have more than one prefix, root, or suffix.
    - Words can be made up of two or more roots:
        - For example: geo + logy
    - Some words have two prefixes:
        - For example: in + sub + ordination
    - Some words have two suffixes:
        - For example: beauti + ful + ly

- Words do not always have a prefix and a suffix.
    - Some words have neither a prefix nor a suffix:
        - For example: read
    - Others have a suffix but no prefix:
        - For example: read + ing
    - Others have a prefix but no suffix:
        - For example: pre + read

- The spelling of roots may change as they are combined with suffixes.

- Different prefixes, roots, or suffixes may have the same meaning.
    - For example: the prefixes bi-, di-, and duo- all mean "two."

- Sometimes you may identify a group of letters as a prefix or root but find that it does not carry the meaning of that prefix or root.
    - For example: the letters "mis" in missile are part of the root but are not the prefix mis-, which means "wrong; bad."

VERBAL WORKSHEETS

Sentence Completions (ISEE)

Sentence Completions Worksheet 1

1. The Three Stooges were a group of physical comedians known for running about and _____ into each other.
   A) colliding
   B) formulating
   C) reveling
   D) correlating

2. The singer's new song was very _____, full of heartfelt lyrics about her recent breakup.
   A) upbeat
   B) earnest
   C) catchy
   D) irate

3. The marketplace was _____ on Saturdays, since people came from all over to shop at the many stalls carrying diverse wares.
   A) barren
   B) desolate
   C) unruly
   D) bustling

4. No river was too wide, no mountain was too _____ for Benjy to conquer; he felt like he could accomplish anything.
   A) shallow
   B) lofty
   C) menial
   D) humble

5. Anjali was _____ when she got her test grade back; she thought she had aced it, but instead she had gotten a D.
   A) thrilled
   B) baffled
   C) composed
   D) elated

6. George Axelrod enjoyed Truman Capote's novella, *Breakfast at Tiffany's*, so much that he decided to write a(n) _____ for the screen.
   A) counterfeit
   B) caricature
   C) adaptation
   D) spoof

7. Marvin stood up from the park bench after finishing his sandwich, and was surprised to find many squirrels _____ nearby, hoping to snatch up his crumbs.
   A) gnawing
   B) scaling
   C) binging
   D) lurking

8. The little baby was very _____, always getting into his mother's drawers and closets.
   A) inquisitive
   B) adorable
   C) dangerous
   D) courageous

9. Although many people have a heightened fear of spiders, most of these creatures _____
   A) are harmless.
   B) are dangerous to humans.
   C) should not be touched.
   D) make people nervous.

10. In 1492, Christopher Columbus sailed across the Atlantic Ocean in two months, a journey that now _____
    A) is possible.
    B) would take 7 hours by airplane.
    C) is seldom undertaken.
    D) takes twice as long to complete.

Sentence Completion Worksheet 2

1. The weekend went by in such a _____, that Cory couldn't even remember what he had done on Saturday.
   A) clatter
   B) whirl
   C) storm
   D) surge

2. Mr. Brand found the painting by the new artist _____, and commissioned him to create a few more for the restaurant's walls.
   A) appalling
   B) distracting
   C) intriguing
   D) homely

3. Mary _____ to her brother that his new suit was appropriate for the wedding, telling him that his suit would match the bridesmaids' dresses.
   A) remarked
   B) yelled
   C) exclaimed
   D) swore

4. Judy's father brought her back a _____ from his business trip to Hawaii.
   A) sea lion
   B) souvenir
   C) reminder
   D) report

5. The professor was _____ by his students for arriving late to his class every day.
   A) encouraged
   B) peeved
   C) stressed
   D) surprised

6. The postman dealt with the _____ dog's barks and snarls for over a year, until he confronted the owners and asked them to control their pet.
   A) gentle
   B) fluffy
   C) offensive
   D) aggressive

7. It is best to turn off the lights when you leave a room, and brush your teeth with the tap off, in order to _____ natural resources.
   A) conserve
   B) keep
   C) reduce
   D) diminish

8. Sacagawea _____ the explorers Lewis and Clark across the western United States, traveling thousands of miles between the years 1804 and 1806.
   A) visited
   B) annoyed
   C) accompanied
   D) explained to

9. George liked to go against the grain, _____
   A) always doing what everyone did.
   B) doing things differently from other people.
   C) spending a lot of time in woodshop class.
   D) causing trouble.

10. I find Ted to be _____, unlike his more tiresome brother Frank.
    A) outgoing but cold
    B) shy and nervous
    C) fun and entertaining
    D) funny and strange

Sentence Completion Worksheet 3

1. High School graduation is a time of revelry and _____, not only for the graduating senior, but also her family and friends.
   A) remembrance
   B) sadness
   C) uncertainty
   D) jubilation

2. Lucy Maud Montgomery's beloved series of books for young adults, Anne of Green Gables, is based upon the titular _____ Anne Shirley.
   A) story
   B) narrative
   C) antagonist
   D) protagonist

3. Even though the mother knew that her children would be messier while she was away for the weekend, she was _____ to find their rooms in such states of disarray.
   A) happy
   B) disgraced
   C) surprised
   D) expecting

4. The student _____ completed his homework, and his grades suffered as a result.
   A) often
   B) seldom
   C) always
   D) normally

5. Vincent Van Gogh was a Dutch painter from the late 1800s, famous for his _____ colors and his similarly bold brushstrokes.
   A) muted
   B) cold
   C) vivid
   D) overwhelming

6. The senator _____ his bid for governor after he admitted that the media reporting on his admittedly poor business practices was true.
   A) prohibited
   B) withdrew
   C) swore
   D) defended

7. The weatherman reported a high _____ of rain on Thursday, the day of Justine's party.
   A) fact
   B) occurrence
   C) perception
   D) probability

8. Environmental activists are concerned about _____ conservation and the saving of natural resources.
   A) history
   B) technology
   C) wilderness
   D) financial

9. Because there was so much traffic on the expressway that evening, Jane was _____.
   A) thrilled that she had a driver's license.
   B) upset that she was late to her brother's piano recital.
   C) unhappy that she would arrive early to class.
   D) disappointed with her bicycle's speed.

10. The American sculptor Alexander Calder is famous both for his delicately balanced mobiles as well as his more _____ stabiles, or grounded metal sculptures.
    A) structured and weighty
    B) light and floating
    C) intricate and dangling
    D) lopsided and boxy

Sentence Completion Worksheet 4

1. The hungry travelers were relieved when they arrived at the _____, the only spot in the desert with water and edible fruits.
   A) dune
   B) peak
   C) cliff
   D) oasis

2. Despite the _____ weather on the day of the picnic, the Perez family enjoyed being outdoors together.
   A) overcast
   B) perfect
   C) sunny
   D) predicted

3. The volcanic eruption of Mt. Vesuvius _____ the Italian city of Pompeii; the architecture is just as it was in the year 79 AD.
   A) saved
   B) ruined
   C) preserved
   D) secured

4. After being stuck next to a talkative woman in the doctor's office waiting room for half an hour, Sean feared he would lose his _____ and moved chairs.
   A) sanity
   B) health
   C) hair
   D) courage

5. There were many _____ to finishing her homework early; Cindy got to watch TV, play basketball with her friends, and eat a snack.
   A) downsides
   B) flaws
   C) benefits
   D) penalties

6. Jordan knew he had upset his mother, so he _____, asking her forgiveness for driving over her flower garden.
   A) begged
   B) repented
   C) retorted
   D) pardoned

7. Max was surprised to see Jamilla _____ on top of the fence, waving down at him.
   A) perching
   B) flying
   C) capering
   D) hobbling

8. Because of the economic _____, people are less likely to buy houses than to rent them.
   A) chaos
   B) stimulus
   C) recession
   D) boom

9. Even though the chef had to improvise many of the ingredients in the stew, he was still able to pull off a _____.
   A) terrible meal
   B) carefully planned menu
   C) delicious feast
   D) mediocre dinner

10. Although Annie Oakley was renowned as a fearsome gunfighter, many first-hand accounts actually describe her as _____.
    A) calm and gentle
    B) cruel and selfish
    C) skilled and cunning
    D) clumsy and greedy

Sentence Completion Worksheet 5

1. When the Ramsey family went camping, they brought a backpack of _____, including canned food, water, and granola bars.
   A) gear
   B) provisions
   C) appliances
   D) trappings

2. Nicola found Asher very _____; he was always getting her to do things that she didn't want to do.
   A) frustrating
   B) considerate
   C) confusing
   D) manipulative

3. Each night when Josephine Baker left the theater, she found many fans _____ by the stage door, waiting for her autograph.
   A) clustered
   B) dispersed
   C) scattered
   D) organized

4. Michaela was upset that her computer _____, seeing as she had only gotten it the month before.
   A) charged
   B) operated
   C) malfunctioned
   D) maneuvered

5. After the first day of soccer tryouts, the coach made a cut; at least half of the aspiring team members were _____.
   A) energized
   B) exhilarated
   C) eliminated
   D) excised

6. Coby had a strong life _____: he believed that everything happened for a reason.
   A) plan
   B) foundation
   C) philosophy
   D) motivation

7. Mrs. Markowitz gave a lot of money to the museum, so the board thanked her for being one of its top _____.
   A) donors
   B) misers
   C) spinsters
   D) opponents

8. Alexis found the bakery window _____; he went inside and spent his last $2 on a cookie.
   A) endearing
   B) creative
   C) irresistible
   D) delicate

9. After a series of thefts, the convenience store installed a video camera to _____.
   A) encourage shoplifters to work more subtly.
   B) monitor activity inside the shop.
   C) animate the atmosphere inside.
   D) dissuade customers from making purchases.

10. The apartment building was closed for disrepair, but was scheduled to be reopened after _____.
    A) the tenants returned.
    B) the interior was damaged.
    C) a series of renovations.
    D) inspection criteria was not met.

Sentence Completion Worksheet 6

1. Mona preferred to keep a healthy diet, but once in a while she would _____ on chocolate croissants.
   A) prey
   B) gorge
   C) advance
   D) grip

2. Each year, the talent show became more and more _____; this past year featured everything from a boy pretending to be a duck, to a group of students dressed as aliens.
   A) enlightening
   B) amusing
   C) bizarre
   D) external

3. The rain beat down so hard that Cheyenne thought it would _____ holes in the roof.
   A) bore
   B) scrape
   C) wield
   D) grapple

4. Notley Manor stood grandly on a manicured lawn that _____ as far as the eye could see.
   A) shrunk
   B) withered
   C) sprawled
   D) leaned

5. Marianna thought that the juice was too _____, so she added water to weaken the taste.
   A) sticky
   B) luscious
   C) fluid
   D) concentrated

6. The Tiny Button Factory _____ buttons, as well as other small home goods.
   A) manufactures
   B) collects
   C) amasses
   D) procures

7. Mrs. Timbers was _____ when she thought her son went missing, but it turned out he was just sitting in a tree, reading a book.
   A) unconcerned
   B) frantic
   C) wary
   D) dangerous

8. Toby found the book so _____ that he finished all eight hundred pages in two days.
   A) unusual
   B) engaging
   C) specific
   D) tedious

9. Jamal feared that there was corruption amidst his fellow officials, because _____.
   A) they were unresponsive to citizens' requests.
   B) he thought he witnessed them accepting bribes.
   C) their work ethic was poor.
   D) all of their speeches were lengthy.

10. Angela screamed and threw a glass at her waiter when her food was prepared incorrectly; the restaurant management told her to never come back _____.
    A) after causing such a commotion.
    B) since the waiter felt ashamed.
    C) for having reveled in her experience.
    D) now that she had alienated her dining companions.

Sentence Completion Worksheet 7

1. Of all Rebecca's _____, getting into college topped the list.
   A) inspirations
   B) imaginings
   C) aspirations
   D) collections

2. No two snowflakes are the same; they might look similar to the naked eye, but they have _____ differences.
   A) massive
   B) stark
   C) minute
   D) extreme

3. Gary loved to tell ghost stories around the campfire, because of the _____ atmosphere they created.
   A) eerie
   B) cozy
   C) solemn
   D) furious

4. Jan knew it was important for an athlete to _____, so she always kept a bottle of water with her.
   A) stretch
   B) hydrate
   C) relax
   D) compete

5. After playing in the woods filled with thorn bushes all day, Marcus's sweatshirt was _____.
   A) wrinkled
   B) matted
   C) tattered
   D) elongated

6. Ashleigh claimed that she was late because of the subway, but she was _____ so often that her teacher didn't believe her.
   A) absent
   B) guilty
   C) excused
   D) tardy

7. Tanya found the map _____; there was no compass rose, and most of the street names had faded away.
   A) bewildering
   B) convincing
   C) revealing
   D) gratifying

8. Although Angelica _____ the crowd for a while, she never caught sight of the friend who was supposed to meet her.
   A) enveloped
   B) surveyed
   C) researched
   D) revered

9. The senator was inspired to create his newest bill, which helped protect endangered species, after _____
   A) collecting votes from his fellow party members.
   B) watching a nature show on television.
   C) aiding the opponents of the environment.
   D) becoming an expert on urban policy.

10. They say that tigers are one of the most ferocious felines in the world, but recently _____.
    A) a man in Kenya trained a tiger to jump through a hoop.
    B) a girl in China tamed a tiger to keep as a pet.
    C) a zookeeper in Boston lost an arm trying to feed a tiger.
    D) a scientist in Turkey found that tigers are more dangerous than lions.

Sentence Completion Worksheet 8

1. The Kargmans finally found the source of the _____ in their living room; a mouse had died under the couch and was starting to decay.
   A) aroma
   B) essence
   C) stench
   D) fragrance

2. Bella felt like she was beginning a new _____ in her life, now that she was starting middle school.
   A) end
   B) chapter
   C) novel
   D) area

3. The look on Nathan's face was difficult to _____; Mina couldn't tell if he was tired or angry.
   A) suspect
   B) overlook
   C) comprehend
   D) monitor

4. Violet decided not to write the speech in advance, because she didn't want to sound _____.
   A) boring
   B) rehearsed
   C) spontaneous
   D) unprepared

5. Ricardo only _____ at the mugger for a moment, so he didn't get a good look at what the man was wearing.
   A) glanced
   B) ogled
   C) gazed
   D) stared

6. The expressway was blocked off for three hours due to the _____ of two cars.
   A) entrance
   B) speeding
   C) maintenance
   D) collision

7. Marni was impressed by Mr. Bingley's _____; it had extensive lawns, a swimming pool, and an orchard.
   A) gazebo
   B) silo
   C) estate
   D) hovel

8. If there was one thing Kresenia was _____ about, it was that she knew her mother would be mad when she saw her bad grades.
   A) certain
   B) unsure
   C) proud
   D) confounded

9. Despite the efforts of the substitute to keep the class in their seats, _____.
   A) the students listened to their iPods.
   B) the students roamed about the classroom.
   C) the students threw paper airplanes from their desks.
   D) the students perched in their chairs.

10. Thanks to a successful mission which put a rover on Mars, _____.
    A) the rover evaporated in space.
    B) we now know that there may once have been life on another planet.
    C) scientists were disappointed by the mission's ineffectiveness.
    D) the astronauts were ridiculed by the press.

Sentence Completion Worksheet 9

1. The high school's Athletic Department is an _____ organization for other student athletic clubs and teams.
   A) overwhelming
   B) active
   C) umbrella
   D) assembling

2. The story Daniel told during lunch was _____ —all about a great adventure and a near-death experience.
   A) tedious
   B) ridiculous
   C) cautionary
   D) epic

3. Alexia didn't think the gold was _____, because the color was rubbing off on parts of the ring.
   A) bright
   B) fake
   C) authentic
   D) artificial

4. There were many _____ in the obstacle course, but Don avoided all of them easily until he got his foot stuck in a tire.
   A) pitfalls
   B) rewards
   C) stages
   D) items

5. When a screw got caught in the gear of a machine, production at the factory was _____ for several days.
   A) enhanced
   B) stalled
   C) furthered
   D) lingered

6. The tree at the top of the hill was old and gnarled, but its branches still _____ skyward.
   A) bowed
   B) hunkered
   C) stretched
   D) drooped

7. The actor had such a big _____, that even his fans got tired of listening to him talk about himself.
   A) voice
   B) persona
   C) ego
   D) personality

8. Although Elisha Kane was a _____ figure during his time, few people today have heard of the man whose funeral was said to have been second only to Lincoln's in size.
   A) unknown
   B) solitary
   C) average
   D) prominent

9. Smallpox was one of the most common contagious diseases in history, until _____.
   A) it continued to spread to other countries.
   B) it was frequent in every population.
   C) scientists created a vaccine to eradicate it.
   D) entire cities were infected.

10. Eating at fancy restaurants was a favorite activity of Robert's friends, but he _____.
    A) had neither the money nor the palate, so he never joined in.
    B) always picked the restaurant, because he was an expert.
    C) enjoyed their weekly dinners immensely.
    D) never cooked, so he preferred to eat out.

Sentence Completion Worksheet 10

1. The last night of sleep-away camp was always _____ ; Katherine and her friends would huddle around the camp fire as they laughed and cried over the events of the summer.
   A) exciting
   B) spooky
   C) emotional
   D) depressing

2. When the bottom of her backpack split open, Amary _____ to collect her papers from the sidewalk before they were blown away.
   A) detained
   B) scrambled
   C) lagged
   D) startled

3. Jeremiah thought his teacher was being rather _____, since she wouldn't listen to his explanation about why he didn't have his homework.
   A) unreasonable
   B) supportive
   C) cruel
   D) terrifying

4. Although ten _____ were interviewed for the job, in the end, only one was selected for the position.
   A) workers
   B) employers
   C) candidates
   D) patrons

5. Ever since Anna clicked on the website, she has been _____ by constant spam emails.
   A) confused
   B) plagued
   C) thrilled
   D) provoked

6. For reasons _____ to Charlie, his mother had decided to paint the living room a hideous shade of green.
   A) unbeknownst
   B) complicated
   C) apparent
   D) muddled

7. The softball team was _____ against the coach, for every player disagreed with his decision to lengthen practices.
   A) separated
   B) battled
   C) yielded
   D) united

8. Rebecca was _____ that the judge's decision would be a favorable one, even though her lawyer didn't have high hopes.
   A) concerned
   B) optimistic
   C) pleased
   D) doubtful

9. The girls on the dance team were considered ruthless and competitive, because _____.
   A) they had long and frequent practices.
   B) their work ethic left something to be desired.
   C) they let nothing stand in the way of winning.
   D) their talent awed everyone at competitions.

10. For all his attempts to avoid confrontation, Donald _____.
   A) got involved in a surprising number of arguments.
   B) always played the peacekeeper.
   C) got along well with everybody.
   D) never had strong opinions.

Sentence Completion Worksheet 11

1. Scientists have found that caffeine in the nectar of some flowers actually _____ the experience for bees, and that the bees are more likely to return to that plant later.
   A) weakens
   B) enhances
   C) corrupts
   D) endangers

2. Douglas thought of Michelle as _____; she always seemed to be in multiple places at the same time.
   A) omnipresent
   B) industrious
   C) aggressive
   D) persevering

3. For being one of the most celebrated playwrights of his day, Tennessee Williams died in an extremely _____ manner – by choking on the cap of some eye medication.
   A) lengthy
   B) mundane
   C) fashionable
   D) aggravated

4. Julie wanted to _____ her _____ notes from all four years of high school Spanish into just one notebook; no easy feat, as there were over 100 pages.
   A) condense .. sparse
   B) consolidate .. copious
   C) augment .. few
   D) collect .. messy

5. The prospective student felt _____ about the University's program in textile design; he was interested in the faculty's expertise in the area, but also disappointed in the lack of diversity in the student body.
   A) ambivalent
   B) puzzled
   C) fervent
   D) anxious

6. The new principal is considered to be very calm and _____, unlike the more _____ principal she replaced.
   A) intense .. anxious
   B) kind .. cautious
   C) serene .. frenzied
   D) collected .. intimidating

7. Even though many are _____ at the thought of speaking in front of large crowds, Laura is actually _____ by this, and finds creativity and energy in the process.
   A) apprehensive .. stimulated
   B) fearful .. terrified
   C) galvanized .. drained
   D) flustered .. relieved

8. Pina Bausch is considered to be one of the most _____ choreographers in the genre of Tanztheater, a style of modern dance that combined dance and theater, and her importance in this field is still honored today.
   A) dramatic
   B) stylized
   C) influential
   D) impotent

9. Lawrence wanted to _____ his annoyance with his tardy friend, as opposed to confront her outright about her lack of _____.
   A) insinuate .. punctuality
   B) intimate .. sincerity
   C) admonish .. capriciousness
   D) verbalize .. consideration

10. Katjana prefers films with a clear message, while Ann finds those movies to be _____ and enjoys more open-ended and _____ films.
    A) inscrutable .. obtuse
    B) annoying .. direct
    C) simpering .. accessible
    D) pedantic .. cryptic

Sentence Completion Worksheet 12

1. The period drama was beautifully filmed, although the film professor was horrified to find many shots included _____ items, like contemporary watches and jewelry.
   A) illicit
   B) clandestine
   C) archaic
   D) anachronistic

2. Although the marathoner appeared to be _____, she admitted that she was actually very tired throughout the race but continued on despite the soreness.
   A) injured
   B) indefatigable
   C) debilitated
   D) exhausted

3. The painter preferred to rely on his _____ color combinations, instead of take risks on techniques with a(n) _____ reception from his peers.
   A) routine .. complimentary
   B) unusual .. guaranteed
   C) standard .. unknown
   D) typical .. decisive

4. The well-trained horse was unaccustomed to the _____ and sudden movements of the _____ rider.
   A) rash .. amateur
   B) inept .. experienced
   C) maladroit .. technical
   D) composed .. novice

5. The class clown liked to _____ people with his pranks, but he avoided anything too extreme that would warrant a suspension.
   A) infuriate
   B) provoke
   C) torment
   D) amuse

6. Martha may say she has a(n)_____ taste in music, but in reality she only listens to music that has been _____ by the critics.
   A) pretentious .. praised
   B) disparaging .. reviewed
   C) singular .. vetted
   D) monotonous .. lauded

7. Though writing letters with pen and paper might seem _____ with today's computers and iPads, many psychologists have found that the act of writing things out by hand actually aids in the task of memorization.
   A) arduous
   B) significant
   C) antiquated
   D) complex

8. The professor found that the article was too _____ to grab the students' attention, so he focused on teaching a more _____ essay on the same topic.
   A) nuanced .. intricate
   B) simplistic .. impenetrable
   C) dry .. accessible
   D) academic .. sardonic

9. My parents like to tell me that I was an exemplary case of an _____ child; I simply could not be controlled and particularly loved to throw tantrums at the grocery store.
   A) obsessive
   B) enervated
   C) inactive
   D) incorrigible

10. The reporter was _____ by the very rude and _____ comments made by the interviewee during the taping.
    A) agitated ..remarkable
    B) flustered .. intriguing
    C) encouraged .. strange
    D) perturbed .. unsettling

Sentence Completion Worksheet 13

1. Post-modernist architect Frank Gehry often cites the _____ of fish as an image that has influenced and populated many of the designs for his buildings and jewelry pieces.
   A) skeleton
   B) motif
   C) composition
   D) scheme

2. Even though the Advil helped to _____ Uma's headache temporarily, the pain returned just an hour later and was actually more_____.
   A) ease .. subtle
   B) relieve .. finite
   C) aggravate .. acute
   D) alleviate .. concentrated

3. Because Zachary became _____ at several points during his interview with the advertising firm, the hiring manager did not think that he could deal with the pressure of the job.
   A) exhausted
   B) flustered
   C) overconfident
   D) aloof

4. Joe was speaking in _____ when he said that he was so hungry he could eat a horse.
   A) hyperbole
   B) metaphor
   C) imagery
   D) code

5. Mary apologized to her sister for borrowing her clothes without asking, but her confession seemed _____ rather than _____.
   A) artificial .. contrite
   B) remorseful .. sorrowful
   C) sincere .. fake
   D) facetious .. genuine

6. The judge _____ lawyers who were clearly fabricating the truth, because he felt like they were undermining the _____ of the judicial system.
   A) encouraged .. bureaucracy
   B) distinguished .. status
   C) abhorred .. integrity
   D) ejected .. flaws

7. Nadia tried to _____ upon her father the importance of being polite to her fiancé's parents, but she wasn't sure the message got through.
   A) enact
   B) impress
   C) persuade
   D) infer

8. The science fiction writer had such a _____ view of the government that he only created _____ and totalitarian worlds as the backdrop for his popular novels.
   A) supportive .. idealistic
   B) keen … haunting
   C) pessimistic .. dystopian
   D) bitter .. picturesque

9. The Millers were concerned that their young son had something of a _____ fascination with road kill; he was frequently _____ for bringing squished squirrels in the house.
   A) intense .. lauded
   B) morose .. upbraided
   C) curious .. scolded
   D) morbid .. lectured

10. The Mennonites reject new technology and _____ clothing; instead, they prefer traditional processes and plain garb.
   A) unembellished
   B) ostentatious
   C) bygone
   D) obsolete

Sentence Completion Worksheet 14

1. Jerry Brown is considered to be a(n) _____ governor, as he openly questions the beliefs and assertions of members of all political parties.
   A) partisan
   B) palliative
   C) iconoclastic
   D) aggressive

2. The teenage daughter found the curfew set by her parents to be _____ and she often _____ by staying out later.
   A) arbitrary .. rebelled
   B) unreasonable ..complied
   C) anonymous .. alleviated
   D) inappropriate .. conciliated

3. The horse-drawn carriages that dot the streets of Amish Pennsylvania appear _____ when contemporary cars speed past them.
   A) modern
   B) anachronistic
   C) altruistic
   D) amorphous

4. The _____ winner of the pie contest created a pie so delicious that even his fellow contestants knew it was clearly the best.
   A) unequivocal
   B) initial
   C) albeit
   D) perfunctory

5. The interviewer considered it to be a(n) _____ mistake on the part of the applicant to fail to send thank you letters within twenty-four hours of the interview, and as a result she has never hired someone who did not follow up with her.
   A) inconsequential
   B) egregious
   C) harmful
   D) noxious

6. The writer could improve his essays if he redacted the _____ and redundant language, leaving behind only the most straightforward and _____ elements.
   A) hyperbolic .. concise
   B) lengthy .. melodramatic
   C) unnecessary .. esoteric
   D) succinct .. edited

7. Jennifer was concerned about the future of the business because she felt like her boss was making decisions based on _____, rather than formulating a plan.
   A) caprice
   B) experience
   C) certitude
   D) innuendo

8. Martin's _____ with sushi was no secret; the deliveryman from the Japanese restaurant was one of his closer _____.
   A) obsession .. nemeses
   B) repulsion .. confidents
   C) fascination .. companions
   D) infatuation .. acquaintances

9. The new girl at school was something of a(n) _____; no one knew where she came from, or why she wore such _____ clothes.
   A) curiosity .. derivative
   B) enigma .. eccentric
   C) mystery .. humdrum
   D) archetype .. atypical

10. The new congressional bill was considered extremely _____, as it addressed practical issues _____ to the general public.
    A) conditional .. pertinent
    B) pragmatic .. relevant
    C) formidable .. appropriate
    D) significant .. extraneous

Sentence Completion Worksheet 15

1. The plaintiff was _____ for her loss, because the judge found her argument valid and her cause _____.
   A) rebuked .. proficient
   B) recouped .. benign
   C) compensated .. sympathetic
   D) berated .. insufficient

2. Jasper approached the newborn _____, having had no prior contact with babies.
   A) exuberantly
   B) gingerly
   C) serenely
   D) adeptly

3. No one was happier than the _____ when the government passed the foreign trade ban, because it secured his _____ on the market.
   A) merchant .. distribution
   B) peddler .. traffic
   C) tycoon .. monopoly
   D) mogul .. impotence

4. The _____ from the novel was confusing, because it didn't provide enough information to establish context.
   A) excerpt
   B) clipping
   C) entity
   D) protagonist

5. The Hornets' coach was known for being _____, but was particularly ill tempered after games when he felt the players ignored his advice.
   A) aloof
   B) irascible
   C) articulate
   D) jovial

6. After a thorough investigation, the _____ was discovered: a raccoon had been _____ the garbage cans on a nightly basis.
   A) source .. augmenting
   B) culprit .. ravaging
   C) prodigy .. wrangling
   D) connoisseur .. ransacking

7. Although her speaking voice was rather _____, Melaena was hailed for her _____ tone when she sang.
   A) gawky .. melodious
   B) melodic .. coarse
   C) strident .. dulcet
   D) musical .. harmonious

8. Robert's teacher _____ his cell phone when she saw him using during class, but she agreed to return it if he aced his test.
   A) banned
   B) dispatched
   C) abducted
   D) confiscated

9. The weekend of partying had not _____ Jasmine much sleep, and she looked _____ when she returned to the office on Monday.
   A) afforded .. haggard
   B) provided .. restless
   C) permitted .. revitalized
   D) allowed .. vigorous

10. Midnight Moon Cheese was a(n) _____ at Westside Market; it was always in stock, no matter the season.
    A) anomaly
    B) staple
    C) phenomenon
    D) element

Sentence Completion Worksheet 16

1. Amelia Earhart was a(n) _____ in the world of aviation; she was the first female pilot to fly solo across the Atlantic Ocean.
   A) founder
   B) orator
   C) pioneer
   D) detractor

2. The town square was _____ at that time of the night, and the empty streets gave it a(n) _____ air.
   A) eerie .. balmy
   B) desolate .. formidable
   C) teeming .. menacing
   D) tranquil .. soothing

3. Mr. Richards ran his household like a military base: he wouldn't stand for tardiness or disobedience, and expected _____ and _____ at every occasion.
   A) exactitude .. anarchy
   B) punctuality .. sedition
   C) exuberance .. agility
   D) promptness .. deference

4. Margaret Thatcher's _____ style as British prime minister defined leadership in a time of hesitation and indecision.
   A) tentative
   B) faltering
   C) unwavering
   D) combative

5. Despite attempts to _____, Avery was unable to stop her little sister from cutting the hair off of all her Barbie dolls.
   A) placate
   B) intervene
   C) chastise
   D) fortify

6. No sooner had Gomez _____ the pipe in his kitchen to stop the leak, that the pipe in his bathroom burst, giving him a new plumbing emergency to _____ with.
   A) fortified .. grapple
   B) repaired .. avail
   C) shackled .. contend
   D) dispatched ., culminate

7. After myriad complaints about the _____ view, city officials finally halted construction on the _____ monument.
   A) derived .. unseemly
   B) enhanced .. titanic
   C) obstructed .. colossal
   D) modified .. picturesque

8. The cabin in the woods was something of a _____ for the family, and they made a monthly retreat from their cramped city apartment.
   A) knoll
   B) haven
   C) novelty
   D) privilege

9. Although she didn't plan on quitting her job for another three months, Camille was already preparing instructions for her _____.
   A) occupant
   B) nemesis
   C) emissary
   D) successor

10. Jared had few _____; in fact, he put so little _____ into any activities that his mother worried he would turn out to be a bum.
    A) ambitions .. optimism
    B) concerns .. impulse
    C) aspirations .. exertion
    D) provisions .. foresight

Sentence Completion Worksheet 17

1. Martha was a(n) _____ host, always welcoming guests into her home with open arms.
   A) robust
   B) pragmatic
   C) gracious
   D) intriguing

2. Though his wife found the beach town _____ and charming, Nathan would have preferred to vacation somewhere less _____, with more access to events and entertainment.
   A) quaint .. remote
   B) secluded .. spacious
   C) thrifty .. restrained
   D) whimsical .. neutral

3. Dora had a strange fascination with all things _____, and her daily routine included a reading of the _____ in the paper.
   A) peculiar .. classifieds
   B) morose .. corrections
   C) primitive .. novelties
   D) macabre .. obituaries

4. Mr. Henderson may have had a deep love of history himself, but his lectures in class did little to _____ the same enthusiasm in his students.
   A) incite
   B) quench
   C) verify
   D) convert

5. Albert Einstein _____ from Germany in 1933, the same year that Adolf Hitler came to power.
   A) dispatched
   B) emigrated
   C) commuted
   D) recuperated

6. Even though her boss said she wouldn't be held _____ for any problems that arose from the new system, everyone in the office blamed Rosalie for the failures after its _____.
   A) responsible .. presentation
   B) hostage .. debut
   C) liable .. implementation
   D) resolute .. distortion

7. Though Muscle Mike wasn't exactly a _____ figure in the wrestling world, everyone enjoyed watching him _____ the reviled Hulking Harry.
   A) popular .. pulverize
   B) anonymous .. decimate
   C) ferocious .. pacify
   D) indelible .. glorify

8. Jemima thought it was _____ that they left town before afternoon, because the hurricane was supposed to arrive that evening.
   A) desperate
   B) probable
   C) misleading
   D) imperative

9. Despite her _____ wish that they leave her alone, the environmentalists with clipboards continued to _____ Donna whenever she walked down her block.
   A) literal .. condemn
   B) express .. badger
   C) eligible .. afflict
   D) bewildering .. abuse

10. The yard sale consisted of a rather _____ collection of articles, from costume jewelry to broken arm chairs.
    A) extravagant
    B) generic
    C) miscellaneous
    D) invaluable

Sentence Completion Worksheet 18

1. Enough research has now been done to prove that climate change is _____, and is not merely a possibility.
   A) urgent
   B) probable
   C) inevitable
   D) synthetic

2. Though Gerald couldn't hear what the people in the conference room were saying, he could see the _____ looks on their faces through the window, and had no desire to enter that _____ environment.
   A) menacing .. hostile
   B) endearing .. rigid
   C) fearful .. potent
   D) gaping .. superficial

3. The scary thing about Lyme disease is that it can have _____ effects – symptoms that don't strike until years after a person contracts the disease.
   A) adverse
   B) latent
   C) immune
   D) negligent

4. Many of the politician's statements were _____, because he chose to follow what he believed in, rather than to _____ to any one party.
   A) haughty .. stoop
   B) inarticulate .. adhere
   C) controversial .. pander
   D) corrosive .. adapt

5. What annoyed the waiter most about his job were the _____ complaints from patrons, who whined about everything from the soap scent in the bathroom to the size of the napkins.
   A) petty
   B) critical
   C) paramount
   D) appalling

6. Jeffery's peers considered him rather _____, always opposing their ideas and arguing with them about any plans they proposed.
   A) eccentric
   B) diplomatic
   C) contrary
   D) inquisitive

7. Pamela was worried that her bad grades might _____ her admittance to college, and was _____ to receive an acceptance letter from one of the schools.
   A) prevent .. perplexed
   B) jeopardize .. relieved
   C) reinforce .. stunned
   D) enhance .. jubilant

8. The remarkable thing about James Bond is that his amazing escapes always seem _____ in the movies, even though there are elements of them that _____ reason.
   A) plausible .. exaggerate
   B) absurd .. imply
   C) feasible .. defy
   D) acceptable .. reinforce

9. Tasha never shared secrets with her coworkers, because she felt like their motives were _____.
   A) confidential
   B) base
   C) public
   D) dubious

10. In the Greek Myth, Achilles is _____ to all injury except on the heel of his foot; the phrase "Achilles' heel" is now commonly used to describe a person's _____.
    A) immune .. vulnerability
    B) susceptible .. weakness
    C) sterile .. exemption
    D) invincible .. vitality

Sentence Completion Worksheet 19

1. Paul Bunyan was known for being a(n) _____ woodsman – he has become a symbol for the big and strong outdoorsman.
   A) adept
   B) gaudy
   C) photogenic
   D) burly

2. Mrs. Marbles was an extremely _____ woman; she was so eager to be involved in other people's business that she sometimes went as far as to _____ their mail!
   A) inconsiderate .. petition
   B) meddlesome .. intercept
   C) tiresome .. obscure
   D) presumptuous .. deliver

3. After several _____ weeks, the citizens of the country were relieved when the fighting ended and a new _____ assumed power.
   A) ungainly .. monarch
   B) tranquil .. oligarch
   C) tumultuous .. regime
   D) violent .. bureaucrat

4. Angelo's tone was always so _____ that none of his friends could ever tell if he actually liked something or if he was just mocking it.
   A) sardonic
   B) introspective
   C) cantankerous
   D) melancholy

5. Even though he had studied Spanish for years, when Christopher went to Barcelona he found the inhabitants completely _____.
   A) foreign
   B) mesmerizing
   C) unintelligible
   D) primitive

6. The delegations at the peace talks found themselves in a _____; no one could agree on anything, but they had promised to have a _____ by the end of the week.
   A) bind .. vendetta
   B) convention .. consensus
   C) conference .. treaty
   D) predicament .. resolution

7. The pilgrims were a(n) _____ group – they prayed several times a day, and their lives revolved around the church.
   A) pious
   B) blasphemous
   C) irreverent
   D) agnostic

8. The musicians _____ fans as they toured from coast to coast; by the time the band reached California, it was _____ across the country.
   A) accrued .. renowned
   B) dispensed .. celebrated
   C) repelled .. notorious
   D) generated .. emitted

9. Naples, FL is one of the most _____ towns in America, and people come from far and wide to glimpse the _____ mansions and fancy sports cars that line the street.
   A) visited .. fortuitous
   B) affluent .. opulent
   C) storied .. grandiose
   D) atypical .. abhorrent

10. Lucas was upset that his science project was disqualified from the competition for a mere _____: he had used the wrong sized font on his otherwise-perfect poster.
    A) omission
    B) transgression
    C) technicality
    D) flaw

Sentence Completion Worksheet 20

1. Marlene _____ to the pressure from her family, and applied to college instead of joining the circus.
   A) adhered
   B) succumbed
   C) converted
   D) collapsed

2. The highway tolls were installed to raise money for the _____ of city roads, but traffic was so backed up as a result, that the action seemed _____.
   A) enhancement .. valuable
   B) betterment .. counterproductive
   C) condemnation .. fruitless
   D) cleansing .. remarkable

3. A judge's greatest challenge is to be both _____ and _____; he or she must listen to the case without prejudice, but then must not hesitate when the time comes for a verdict.
   A) unbiased .. decisive
   B) opinionated .. absolute
   C) dynamic .. contemplative
   D) cautious .. forceful

4. Sometimes, when Rebecca was bored in class, she would _____ her peers and imagine what they would all be doing in twenty years.
   A) snub
   B) condone
   C) survey
   D) fabricate

5. Compared to all the troubles in the world, Cathy's _____ about her hair seemed _____ when put into perspective.
   A) gripes .. implausible
   B) regret .. shameful
   C) concerns .. trivial
   D) contentment .. valid

6. Natalia thought the "Keep Out" sign posted on the house's gate was somewhat _____, seeing as there was a snarling Rottweiler chained to a post outside the door, as well.
   A) threatening
   B) redundant
   C) imposing
   D) contradictory

7. After the witness _____ the information to the detectives, they were able to _____ the case in a short time.
   A) revealed .. abandon
   B) withheld .. resolve
   C) confessed .. scrutinize
   D) disclosed .. settle

8. AJ thought the candy tasted pretty _____, despite the packaging's claim that it was "made from real fruit."
   A) abhorrent
   B) succulent
   C) artificial
   D) counterfeit

9. The townsfolk loved when the travelling players came to town, because the shows provided a(n) _____ from the _____ of daily life.
   A) escape .. solace
   B) diversion .. drudgery
   C) respite .. wonders
   D) supplement .. toils

10. Many of Mary Shelley's works are _____ with sadness, because she never quite recovered from the loss of two of her children.
    A) deluged
    B) tinged
    C) saturated
    D) distorted

SENTENCE COMPLETION ANSWER KEY

Worksheet 1
1. A
2. B
3. D
4. B
5. B
6. C
7. D
8. A
9. A
10. B

Worksheet 2
1. B
2. C
3. A
4. B
5. B
6. D
7. A
8. C
9. B
10. C

Worksheet 3
1. D
2. D
3. C
4. B
5. C
6. B
7. D
8. C
9. B
10. A

Worksheet 4
1. D
2. A
3. C
4. A
5. C
6. B
7. A
8. C
9. C
10. A

Worksheet 5
1. B
2. D
3. A
4. C
5. C
6. C
7. A
8. C
9. B
10. C

Worksheet 6
1. B
2. C
3. A
4. C
5. D
6. A
7. B
8. B
9. B
10. A

Worksheet 7
1. C
2. C
3. A
4. B
5. C
6. D
7. A
8. B
9. B
10. B

Worksheet 8
1. C
2. B
3. C
4. B
5. A
6. D
7. C
8. A
9. B
10. B

Worksheet 9
1. C
2. D
3. C
4. A
5. B
6. C
7. C
8. D
9. C
10. A

Worksheet 10
1. C
2. B
3. A
4. C
5. B
6. A
7. D
8. B
9. C
10. A

Worksheet 11
1. B
2. A
3. B
4. B
5. A
6. C
7. A
8. C
9. A
10. D

Worksheet 12
1. D
2. B
3. C
4. A
5. B
6. C
7. C
8. C
9. D
10. D

Worksheet 13
1. B
2. D
3. B
4. A
5. D
6. C
7. B
8. C
9. D
10. B

Worksheet 14
1. C
2. A
3. B
4. A
5. B
6. A
7. A
8. D
9. B
10. B

Worksheet 15
1. C
2. B
3. C
4. A
5. B
6. B
7. C
8. D
9. A
10. B

Worksheet 16
1. C
2. D
3. D
4. C
5. B
6. A
7. C
8. B
9. D
10. C

Worksheet 17
1. C
2. A
3. D
4. A
5. B
6. C
7. A
8. D
9. B
10. C

Worksheet 18
1. C
2. A
3. B
4. C
5. A
6. C
7. B
8. C
9. D
10. A

Worksheet 19
1. D
2. B
3. C
4. A
5. C
6. D
7. A
8. A
9. B
10. C

Worksheet 20
1. B
2. B
3. A
4. C
5. C
6. B
7. D
8. C
9. B
10. B

Analogies (SSAT)

Analogies Worksheet 1

1. Lamp: light
   A) ball: air
   B) sleeve: sweater
   C) tree: shade
   D) window: glass
   E) shell: shore

2. Historian: history
   A) plumber: pipes
   B) dog: bark
   C) priest: church
   D) choir: organ
   E) doctor: medicine

3. Principal: school
   A) president: country
   B) building: architect
   C) beaver: dam
   D) nurse: hospital
   E) machine: factory

4. Creepy: terrifying
   A) calm: tranquil
   B) annoyed: furious
   C) hideous: unattractive
   D) torturous: painful
   E) fortunate: lucky

5. Ship: ocean
   A) car: garage
   B) airplane: airport
   C) train: railroad
   D) bird: nest
   E) cart: horse

6. Starving: food
   A) happy: money
   B) confused: information
   C) comfortable: safety
   D) noisy: din
   E) removed: space

7. Actor: performance
   A) athlete: practice
   B) fireman: fire
   C) ranger: forest
   D) jockey: horse
   E) professor: lecture

8. Labrador: dog
   A) cobra: snake
   B) mailman: post office
   C) kitten: cat
   D) squirrel: acorn
   E) grocery: vegetable

9. Focused: distracted
   A) affluent : wealthy
   B) motivated: interested
   C) active: upset
   D) frigid: warm
   E) constructive: accomplished

10. Farm: food
    A) cow: milk
    B) phone: message
    C) book: pages
    D) classroom: pencils
    E) internet: computer

Analogies Worksheet 2

1. Sweater: wool
   A) bird: wings
   B) child: school
   C) jar: glass
   D) teeth: mouth
   E) diamond: earring

2. Seat: bus
   A) water: lake
   B) coat: closet
   C) garden: flower
   D) drink: ice cube
   E) wheel: wagon

3. Distant: near
   A) empty: vacant
   B) encouraging: clever
   C) sympathetic: kind
   D) lofty: grounded
   E) brave: heroic

4. Ballerina: dancer
   A) athlete: soccer player
   B) biographer: writer
   C) aunt: uncle
   D) reporter: tv camera
   E) boss: owner

5. Scholar: knowledgeable
   A) millionaire: generous
   B) runner: unhealthy
   C) spy: secretive
   D) soldier: aggressive
   E) servant: liberated

6. Sapling: tree
   A) skyscraper: building
   B) clown : circus
   C) gopher: hole
   D) tadpole: frog
   E) stanza: poem

7. Catastrophe: problem
   A) protection: safety
   B) elation: gladness
   C) energy: exhaustion
   D) craft: skill
   E) leader: dictator

8. Column: roof
   A) leg: tabletop
   B) mask: face
   C) elevator: stairs
   D) painting: easel
   E) binder: ring

9. Violin: music
   A) house: builder
   B) fireplace: warmth
   C) flower: seed
   D) suitcase: luggage
   E) chin: frown

10. Sitcom: television
    A) costume: opera
    B) sport: tennis
    C) ballad: song
    D) chapter: novel
    E) utensil: fork

Analogies Worksheet 3

1. Fiction: fact
   A) forest: pine
   B) run: jog
   C) ounce: pound
   D) joy: despair
   E) chart: diagram

2. Earplugs: noise
   A) roadblocks: cars
   B) horn: bell
   C) barrier: dam
   D) notes: trumpet
   E) drain: water

3. Slumber: doze
   A) waken: energize
   B) leap: hop
   C) fly: dive
   D) dream: imagine
   E) sketch: paint

4. Match: flame
   A) lead: pencil
   B) thread: needle
   C) tie: shirt
   D) ignition: car
   E) crown: head

5. Branch: tree
   A) arm: leg
   B) cup: saucer
   C) bumper: truck
   D) flower: petal
   E) mustache: hair

6. Axe: woodsman
   A) siren: ambulance
   B) saw: architect
   C) acrobat: trapeze
   D) pen: writer
   E) sculpture: metal

7. Helpless: capable
   A) optimistic: pessimistic
   B) retired: old
   C) angry: irate
   D) strong: boney
   E) flexible: easy

8. Minute: hour
   A) time: years
   B) grass: blade
   C) button: hole
   D) finger: nail
   E) room: hotel

9. Box: corner
   A) apple: leaf
   B) brick: clay
   C) glass: shard
   D) spout: jug
   E) star: point

10. Anxious: worried
   A) calm: tired
   B) soft: loud
   C) enthusiastic: exuberant
   D) clear: crafty
   E) forgetful: sharp

Analogies Worksheet 4

1. Chef: kitchen
    A) electrician: wires
    B) surgery: doctor
    C) policeman: uniform
    D) teacher: classroom
    E) driver: garage

2. Ant: insect
    A) river: stream
    B) rat: rodent
    C) cloud: storm
    D) feline: cat
    E) foal: horse

3. Umbrella: shade
    A) pillow: comfort
    B) car: journey
    C) shoe: lace
    D) sight: glasses
    E) numbers: calculation

4. Amusing: hysterical
    A) smelly: aroma
    B) smooth: rough
    C) allow: permit
    D) hungry: ravenous
    E) interesting: fascinating

5. Celebrity: famous
    A) mall: busy
    B) protester: calm
    C) engine: complex
    D) box: compact
    E) millionaire: wealthy

6. Unhealthy: nutritious
    A) cold: hot
    B) boring: noble
    C) tired: exhausted
    D) hard: solid
    E) curious: strange

7. Rain: wet
    A) wind: comfortable
    B) sandpaper: rough
    C) leaf: crunchy
    D) curtain: heavy
    E) shoelace: knotted

8. Encourage: inspire
    A) remove: replace
    B) compose: write
    C) lengthen: condense
    D) applaud: convince
    E) battle: agree

9. Egg: yolk
    A) oil: water
    B) button: coat
    C) milk: carton
    D) rose: vase
    E) light bulb: filament

10. Kite: fly
    A) guitar: strum
    B) cruise: float
    C) ball: bounce
    D) frying pan: burn
    E) hood: camouflage

Analogies Worksheet 5

1. Crazy: sanity
   A) popular: support
   B) significant: importance
   C) ignorant: knowledge
   D) strong: muscle
   E) shy: timidity

2. Dowdy: stylish
   A) remarkable: ordinary
   B) clever: intelligent
   C) harmful: cruel
   D) delicious: tasty
   E) thirsty: painful

3. Peacock: bird
   A) colorful: painting
   B) tiger: lion
   C) marsupial: koala
   D) banner: flag
   E) lizard: reptile

4. Artist: creative
   A) builder: constructive
   B) politician: ambitious
   C) scientist: chemical
   D) director: motivated
   E) cashier: eager

5. Awkward: clunky
   A) small: piecemeal
   B) cheerful: dazzling
   C) nervous: apprehensive
   D) kind: ignorant
   E) flashy: simple

6. Teeth: chew
   A) arms: swing
   B) flowers: wilt
   C) scissors: cut
   D) knees: knock
   E) ropes: tie

7. Large: gigantic
   A) cynical: trustworthy
   B) smoky: misty
   C) rational: emotional
   D) classic: old-fashioned
   E) attractive: gorgeous

8. Musician: orchestra
   A) journalist: column
   B) photographer: camera
   C) clown: circus
   D) nanny: children
   E) butcher: meat

9. Shoe store: sneakers
   A) gift shop: souvenirs
   B) laundromat: clothes
   C) bank: savings
   D) military: soldiers
   E) bakery: groceries

10. Temperature: degrees
    A) mile: meters
    B) weight: pounds
    C) heat: warm
    D) volume: liquid
    E) seconds: time

1. Enthusiastic: apathetic
   A) notorious: infamous
   B) rational: intelligent
   C) compulsory: optional
   D) capable: ambiguous
   E) functional: efficient

2. Lobster: shellfish
   A) cougar: mountain lion
   B) fracture: injury
   C) drawing: cartoon
   D) vacuum: mop
   E) churn: butter

3. Weed: garden
   A) yeast: bread
   B) frame: portrait
   C) mold: fungus
   D) cloud: sky
   E) termite: wood

4. Patron: supporter
   A) artist: painter
   B) physician: healer
   C) teacher: genius
   D) leader: mayor
   E) prisoner: snitch

5. Roe: fish
   A) cat: kitten
   B) manatee: whale
   C) larva: insect
   D) cocoon: moth
   E) falcon: hawk

6. Congregant: church
   A) policeman: squad
   B) politician: office
   C) army: platoon
   D) scientist: lab
   E) model: magazine

7. Reimburse: compensate
   A) fracture: solidify
   B) malign: praise
   C) acclimate: resume
   D) forgo: concede
   E) rephrase: stutter

8. Concerned: panicked
   A) remote: removed
   B) sad: inconsolable
   C) passionate: invested
   D) dangerous: frightening
   E) alert: cautious

9. Blood: artery
   A) dam: reservoir
   B) pump: well
   C) sky: airplane
   D) subway car: tunnel
   E) ledge: balcony

10. Yarn: sweater
    A) shoes: laces
    B) batter: ingredients
    C) democracy: votes
    D) dance: musical
    E) shingle: roof

Analogies Worksheet 7

1. Tropical: climate
   A) temperate: continent
   B) arid: desert
   C) perennial: flower
   D) equatorial: oasis
   E) arboreal: field

2. Destructive: restorative
   A) pensive: thoughtful
   B) climactic: cautionary
   C) wistful: disgruntled
   D) comely: hideous
   E) sage: wise

3. Zealot: enthusiast
   A) pauper: miser
   B) reactionary: conservative
   C) cadet: lieutenant
   D) benefactor: contributor
   E) invader: pacifist

4. Detective: clues
   A) lawyer: litigation
   B) paleontologist: bones
   C) psychiatrist: medication
   D) economist: bonds
   E) publicist: anonymity

5. Drizzle: deluge
   A) cloud: haze
   B) tornado: hurricane
   C) blizzard: dusting
   D) fog: mist
   E) breeze: gust

6. Humidifier: moisture
   A) fire: smoke
   B) silo: grain
   C) faucet: sink
   D) weapon: armory
   E) spade: ditch

7. Necklace: jewelry
   A) cravat: tie
   B) shoe: espadrille
   C) wrap: shawl
   D) glove: muff
   E) monocle: hat

8. Foundation: building
   A) quilt: stitch
   B) production: company
   C) wick: candle
   D) bulb: flower
   E) yacht: sail

9. Stingy: thrifty
   A) eloquent: verbose
   B) heralded: lauded
   C) urgent: tardy
   D) extreme: norm
   E) active: lethargic

10. Ignored: attention
    A) picturesque: beauty
    B) disdained: energy
    C) magnanimous: greed
    D) covert: stealth
    E) productive: materials

Analogies Worksheet 8

1. Labyrinth: complex
   A) estate: private
   B) insight: secluded
   C) neighborhood: guarded
   D) epiphany: mundane
   E) entourage: threatening

2. Arson: crime
   A) quotation: truism
   B) ammonia: chemical
   C) platoon: ship
   D) speed: destination
   E) paddle: canoe

3. Surplus: lack
   A) emergency: upheaval
   B) routine: continuity
   C) pronouncement: acclaim
   D) faith: skepticism
   E) ease: liberation

4. Mother: nurture
   A) government: regulate
   B) brother: inherit
   C) salesman: connive
   D) monster: descend
   E) thug: surprise

5. Melodrama: histrionic
   A) comedy: tragedy
   B) irony: dramatic
   C) cinematic: film
   D) classic: ancient
   E) farce: campy

6. Astronaut: shuttle
   A) submarine: navy
   B) meteorologist: balloon
   C) explorer: quest
   D) sailor: schooner
   E) seer: crystal ball

7. Vulnerable: susceptible
   A) aggravating: morbid
   B) pungent: bland
   C) amateur: unprofessional
   D) accomplished: earnest
   E) marketable: inaccessible

8. Pundit: expert
   A) official: judge
   B) prodigy: success
   C) mentor: guide
   D) luminary: precursor
   E) activist: writer

9. Column: newspaper
   A) car: gear
   B) disposal: trash
   C) frame: photograph
   D) mug: handle
   E) tile: mosaic

10. Creative: derivative
    A) jealous: envious
    B) accurate: imprecise
    C) succinct: curt
    D) unpleasant: cordoned
    E) obnoxious: frivolous

Analogies Worksheet 9

1. Tone-deaf: pitch
   A) grounded: humility
   B) forgetful: memory
   C) popular: friends
   D) shallow: exterior
   E) morose: feeling

2. Envision: foresee
   A) esteem: respect
   B) fantasize: realize
   C) respond: deter
   D) mature: spread
   E) infer: explain

3. Martyr: sacrifice
   A) hero: warrior
   B) blacksmith: mallet
   C) broadcaster: announcement
   D) poet: volume
   E) matriarch: insight

4. Microscope: magnify
   A) curtain: gingham
   B) pedal: steer
   C) net: capture
   D) cleanse: bleach
   E) mirror: obscure

5. Pedicure: toes
   A) kidneys: dialysis
   B) amputation: leg
   C) brace: back
   D) skin: facial
   E) massage: muscles

6. Shrewd: canny
   A) marketable: expensive
   B) pliable: limber
   C) trustworthy: sly
   D) charismatic: blunt
   E) authoritative: meek

7. Triumph: failure
   A) contract: agreement
   B) nerves: agitation
   C) forgiveness: grudge
   D) competition: creation
   E) fervor: passion

8. Stone: jade
   A) iguana: lizard
   B) wicker: basket
   C) bugle: instrument
   D) bird: buzzard
   E) song: tempo

9. Fade: blackout
   A) light: glare
   B) warm: boil
   C) crease: fold
   D) stretch: bend
   E) diminish: surge

10. Drowsy: energy
    A) humorless: wit
    B) striking: plain
    C) cultured: experience
    D) wealthy: affluence
    E) emotional: sense

Analogies Worksheet 10

1. Tent: shelter
   A) hammock: shade
   B) truck: distance
   C) phone: talk
   D) salad: nourishment
   E) cellar: moisture

2. Contrary: agreeable
   A) faulty: flawed
   B) ancient: diminished
   C) functional: efficient
   D) exalted: inventive
   E) privileged: prosperous

3. Producer: movies
   A) foreman: factories
   B) diplomat: negotiations
   C) fisherman: catch
   D) teacher: classrooms
   E) rock star: throngs

4. Splashed: soaked
   A) brushed: rammed
   B) concealed: hid
   C) imagined: dreamed
   D) choked: coughed
   E) froze: animated

5. Soldier: marches
   A) captain: feigns
   B) watchman: hunts
   C) contortionist: climbs
   D) conductor: trains
   E) ballerina: twirls

6. Contention: conflict
   A) essence: core
   B) clarity: obstruction
   C) recognition: clamor
   D) modification: simplicity
   E) introduction: summary

7. Marionette: puppet
   A) comet: planet
   B) act: circus
   C) conch: shell
   D) bucket: well
   E) curtain: fringe

8. Immoral: ethics
   A) constructive: resources
   B) educated: instruction
   C) wild: restrictions
   D) productive: willpower
   E) encouraged: support

9. Paragraph: essay
   A) knot: string
   B) character: foil
   C) cabinet: collection
   D) chorus: song
   E) drawer: handle

10. Exotic: foreign
    A) noble: regal
    B) playful: lavish
    C) scholarly: rehearsed
    D) spirited: destitute
    E) ostentatious: modest

ANALOGIES WORKSHEETS
ANSWER KEY

Worksheet 1
1. C
2. E
3. A
4. B
5. C
6. B
7. E
8. A
9. D
10. A

Worksheet 2
1. C
2. E
3. D
4. B
5. C
6. D
7. B
8. A
9. B
10. C

Worksheet 3
1. D
2. A
3. B
4. D
5. C
6. D
7. A
8. E
9. E
10. C

Worksheet 4
1. D
2. B
3. A
4. D
5. E
6. A
7. B
8. B
9. E
10. C

Worksheet 5
1. C
2. A
3. E
4. B
5. C
6. C
7. E
8. C
9. A
10. B

Worksheet 6
1. C
2. B
3. E
4. B
5. C
6. A
7. D
8. B
9. D
10. E

Worksheet 7
1. C
2. D
3. D
4. B
5. E
6. A
7. A
8. C
9. B
10. C

Worksheet 8
1. A
2. B
3. D
4. A
5. E
6. D
7. C
8. C
9. E
10. B

Worksheet 9

1. B
2. A
3. C
4. C
5. E
6. B
7. C
8. D
9. B
10. A

Worksheet 10

1. D
2. B
3. B
4. A
5. E
6. A
7. C
8. C
9. D
10. A

Essay Strategies

ISEE ESSAY TIPS

The ISEE essay is timed and written in response to a creative prompt. This essay is not scored; it is scanned and sent only to the schools you requested.

ISEE Lower Level Example prompts
- Describe your perfect day.
- How could we make the world a nicer place to live?
- Who is your favorite family member and why?
- Where would you spend your perfect vacation?

ISEE Middle Level Example prompts
- How could you improve your community?
- What is a career that you would like to pursue one day?
- What is one problem facing the world today and how could it be solved?
- What is a personal experience that has inspired you?
- If you could have a super power, what would it be and why?

ISEE Upper Level Example prompts
- Is change the hardest thing?
- What is your favorite book and why?
- Name someone you admire. What about them makes them admirable?
- If you needed to perform community service, what type would you pick and why?
- What makes a person "successful"? Explain, using a specific example.

Write a 5-paragraph essay. Schools teach students to write essays with good organization, and usually that means a standard 5-paragraph essay. Organization is so important to the ISEE that they put the word "organize" in their official instructions. Start with a short introduction, then include 3 paragraphs explaining WHY you chose your answer to the prompt, and then end with a conclusion.

- Don't start writing unless you have a clear outline.
- Don't worry about the length of each paragraph; 4-5 sentences is fine for each of the example paragraphs, and 1-2 sentences is fine for the Introduction and the Conclusion.
- Always strive to be concise and clear. Avoid "filler." You don't need to add unnecessary length, as it is your content that is most important.
- Check to see that your points are clear.
- Save time to proofread.

Time Organization
- 5 minutes – Read the prompt and plan out your essay.
- 20 minutes – Write your essay.

- 5 minutes – Re-read your essay and proofread.

Introduction Tips
- Make the first sentence of the introduction a "grabber." A grabber can be any of the following:
  - A question
  - A quotation
  - An anecdote (a brief story about something that the student has experienced)
  - A vivid description
- Make sure that your grabber is relevant to the prompt.
- In the introduction, you should also be very clear about your stance on the topic.

Body Paragraphs
- Explain and elaborate on the arguments you listed in your introduction. It is generally a good idea to arrange your body paragraphs in the same order in which the arguments appear in the introduction.
- Each body paragraph should begin with a topic sentence.
- All information in a body paragraph should explain and support the topic sentence.
- Each body paragraph should end with a concluding sentence that wraps up the paragraph and restates the reason.

Conclusion
- In the conclusion, you should restate your position and arguments, but without using the exact same wording used in the introduction.
- End with a strong closing sentence that neatly sums up your essay.

SSAT Essay Tips

Upper Level SSAT Prompts
In the Writing section, the students must choose between a creative prompt and an essay prompt.
- If a student decides to respond to the creative prompt, the response must also be creative and make use of animated explanations. The creative prompt might be ambiguous and require the students to build the entire essay almost by themselves.
- When responding to the essay prompt, students must use strong examples from the text to support their answers.

Middle Level SSAT Prompt
Both of the two Writing prompts are creative. The response to the prompts must also be creative and make use of animated explanations. Students are expected to use grammar and vocabulary which conform to Standard English.

ESSAY:
Each essay question consists of a topic (short phrase, proverb, or question) and an assignment (usually to agree or disagree with the position taken). There is no right or wrong answer.

Some examples:
- Is it more important to learn from mistakes or from successes?
- Which are more important, arts and music or sports and athletics?
- What three qualities define a good student?
- What is the most important issue facing the world today and what would you do to contribute to solving this issue?

Tips:

1) **Stick to the topic:** So many students go off on tangents instead of discussing the topic. Rephrase the question in your own words to make sure you understand what it is asking you. You may be creative in your approach, but you need to take a clear position and support that position with specific examples from your own experience, the experience of others, current events, literature, or history.

2) **Plan the essay:** Write an outline first. Planning makes the writing process easier, faster, and more organized. Allow 3-5 minutes to decide on stance, brainstorm two to three examples that support the thesis, and make a brief outline for a 3-5 paragraph essay. Allow 15 minutes to write the essay as neatly and legibly as possible. Allow approximately 5 minutes to revise and proofread your essay.

3) **Show – don't tell:** Rather than explaining why you believe a statement is true or not, use relevant examples that illustrate the point that you want to make. Preferably, avoid examples from your personal life.

4) **Grammar, punctuation, and sentence structure:** Check for two of the most common errors: sentence fragments and run-on sentences. Avoid monotony by varying the rhythm and length of your sentences.

5) **Word choice:** Check for the overused words – "things" and "stuff". Replace words that do not add quality to your essay with more detailed, advanced academic vocabulary. Use exciting verbs to empower your writing. Also, check for pronouns (him, her, they, it) that have no antecedent.

6) **Legibility:** Write or print so that the writing is legible. Edit carefully, just putting striking through a word or phrase that you revise.

CREATIVE:

1) **Pre-write your essay:** The creative essay prompt is open-ended. For example, the prompt "And then she came in the door…" could be the beginning of an essay about almost anything you choose. Your essay could be about a friend, sibling, teacher, mother, detective, etc. Other examples of creative prompts are:

- "He couldn't believe they wanted his help…"
- "The silence was deafening…"
- "He was hanging on by a thread…"

The possibilities are endless. Try writing a creative essay in advance that could be adaptable to a variety of prompts. Do some research on a favorite subject, or think about a personal accomplishment that you would like an admissions officer to know about. Hopefully, you can adapt this idea to a creative prompt on test day.

2) **Writing a story:** If you use the creative prompt to write a story, start with some tension and immediacy (the unusual, the unexpected, an action or conflict) to grab the reader's attention. A good story has a conflict, a climax (when the rising action of the story reaches its peak) and a resolution (conflict is resolved). In 25 minutes, it is difficult to provide a complete resolution, but you want to reveal that the characters are beginning to change or are starting to see things differently.

3) **Words/Imagery:** Your goal should be clear, lively writing that employs imagery and well-chosen vocabulary that shows rather than tells. For example, instead of writing that Linda was scared, you could write that her hands were clammy or that her body was quivering like a bowl of jello. Instead of writing that John asked the question nervously, you could write – "Where are you going?" John stammered, staring at his sneakers. Make it riveting! Avoid he said, she said. Reveal a character's tone; for example, "….she snorted in amusement…" or "…he asked contemptuously…"

CHAPTER 4: STUDENT PAGES

Homework Assignments

NOTES

About Private Prep

Private Prep is an education services company that offers individually customized lessons in all K-12 academic subjects, standardized test prep, and college admissions consulting. We believe personal attention is fundamental to critical to academic achievement and lies at the forefront of every student-tutor relationship. Designing curriculum for each student's unique learning style, we focus not only on improving grades and increasing test scores, but also on building confidence and developing valuable skills—like work ethic, growth mindset, and anxiety management—that will last a lifetime.

One of the most significant points of differentiation between us and other educational services companies is our team approach. Our directors work in tandem with tutors and support staff to provide comprehensive, collaborative support to families.

We also focus on giving back to the communities in which we work. Through the Private Prep Scholarship Program, we place high-achieving students from low-income or underserved backgrounds with individual tutors, who work with them to navigate the test prep and college application process and ultimately gain admission to best-fit colleges.

At Private Prep, we deliver a superior academic experience—in the U.S., abroad, and online—that is supported by diverse and excellent resources in recruitment, curriculum design, professional training, and custom software development.

12.08.2020 1748